LOVE, SEX AND TRACTORS

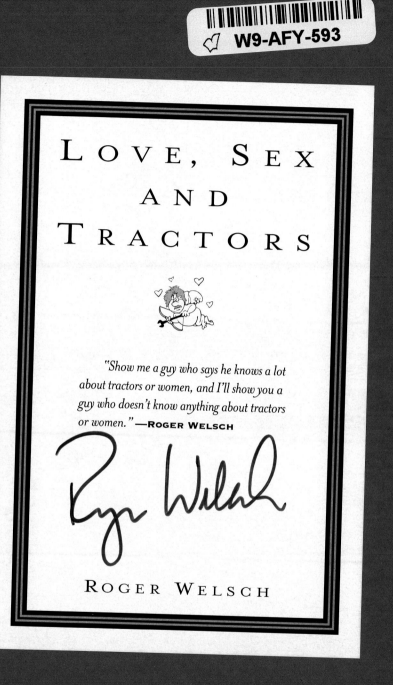

"Show me a guy who says he knows a lot about tractors or women, and I'll show you a guy who doesn't know anything about tractors or women." —**ROGER WELSCH**

ROGER WELSCH

LOVE, SEX AND TRACTORS

THE ETERNAL TRIANGLE

LOVE, SEX AND TRACTORS

THE ETERNAL TRIANGLE

ROGER WELSCH

MBI Publishing Company

First published in 2000 by MBI Publishing Company, 729 Prospect Avenue,
PO Box 1, Osceola, WI 54020-0001 USA

The information in this book is true and complete to the best of our
knowledge. All recommendations are made without any guarantee on the part of
the author or Publisher, who also disclaim any liability incurred in connection
with the use of this data or specific details.

We recognize that some words, model names and designations, for example,
mentioned herein are the property of the trademark holder. We use them for
identification purposes only. This is not an official publication.

MBI Publishing Company books are also available at discounts in bulk quantity
for industrial or sales-promotional use. For details write to Special Sales
Manager at Motorbooks International Wholesalers & Distributors,
729 Prospect Avenue, PO Box 1, Osceola, WI 54020-0001 USA.

Library of Congress Cataloging-in-Publication Data Available
    Welsch, Roger L.
        Love, sex and tractors / Roger Welsch
            p. cm.
        Includes index.
        ISBN: 0-7603-0998-1 (hardbound. : alk. paper)
            1. Tractors—Maintenance and repair—Popular works. 2. Farm tractors
—Conservation and restoration—Popular works. I. Title.
    TL233.25 . W42 2000
    629.22'2—dc21

Acquisitions Editor: Lee Klancher
Content Editor: Paula Barbour
Cover & Text Designer: Tom Heffron

Printed in China

CONTENTS

DEDICATION

F or the love interests in my life, the tall and short, reedy and stout, pretty and plain, tender and tough, green, red, or Persian orange—you may be just old iron to others, but to me you are all, each one, an objet d'amour.

Hell hath no fury like a woman. Forget the part about "scorned."
—GEORGE SCHWELLE, VISIONS

ACKNOWLEDGMENTS

Everyone hates it when some actor gets an award and stands at the mike reciting the name of every producer, gaffer, or best boy who worked on the production for which he or she is getting the trophy. But you know, what they are saying is true: It really couldn't have been done without them. So pay attention now, and read the names below. I'm not just wasting your time. These folks really did have a lot to do with this book, and I really couldn't have done it without them. It would only be discreet not to list the names of those who have instructed me in the ways of love and romance, and maybe even a matter of survival, since Linda is going to read this. But I will thank her, not only for her love, but for her forbearance and patience. It can't be easy.

I owe the most to Dan Selden and Dennis "Bondo" Adams. When they come over here and spend a full, hard day working at getting one of my "restorations" started, I am left at the end of the day wondering why they did it. Okay, there were two cases of cold beer in the cooler, but still, they could've been sitting in the shade at some farm pond watching a bobber. I am amazed again and again at all they know, and I appreciate their friendship. Next round's on me, boys.

Don Hochstetler, Al Schmitt, Melvin Nelson, Melvin Halsey, and Kenny Porath are real mechanics. It's got to be painful for them to see me dinking around, doing really stupid stuff, but they are (for the most part) patient, and don't laugh and point their fingers until I am out their doors and down the street a ways. I envy their knowledge and thank them for their generosity.

There's another batch of mechanic friends who've helped me, but whom I've never met: all the posters over at the ATIS antique tractor site on the worldwide web. They're the reason I have the chapter in this book about cybermechanics. Imagine how convenient it is to have a question, serious or goofy, and simply type it onto a screen, post it at the ATIS site, and soon have a dozen authoritative answers coming back! A lot of your words are in these pages, cyberbuddies.

Bud and Pat Stoeger, Dale Duncan, and Mick Maun have always been cheerful and helpful when I've asked them for their help. Phil Hinrichs up at the post office and Scott Leisinger, our faithful UPS man, deliver more good humor than packages most of the time, and smile even when they are unloading a box containing an anvil or floor jack. I especially appreciate their cooperation in keeping Linda from finding out about half the stuff I buy from the catalogs.

When it comes to hardware, parts, products, tools, that kind of thing, I owe a debt of gratitude to Kevin and Wayne Hilder over at the Allis-Chalmers dealership in Central City. Imagine running a business where you are trying to sell the latest technology on the market and a guy comes in looking for a part for a machine that was built before the salesman was born! The Hilders have always shown an interest in and support for my tractor projects. They are great folks and good friends.

A good part of *Busted Tractors and Rusty Knuckles* was about my buddy Jim Stromp, who runs a tractor salvage yard near Spalding, Nebraska, about an hour north of my home in Dannebrog. Jim is a friend and an authentic character. Jim, I am grateful for all your help.

Ben Campbell of Rusty Iron Farm, a guy who knows his way around tool folks, and Ted Metzger at Intertec, publisher of the absolutely indispensable I&T shop guides for tractors, have been unexpected benefactors in my tractor work. Same with Leigh Dorrington of Pendine Motorsports Group and Bill DeArment of ChannelLock. Long ago I stopped believing in Santa Claus, but recently I've come to believe in the workshop elves Ben

Campbell, Ted Metzger, Leigh Dorrington, and Bill DeArment.

Paula Barbour and Dave Mowitz at *Successful Farming* magazine have been helpful in a dozen ways—more often cheerleading than mechanical—but I don't think I could have survived in life, love, or tractors without them. You guys have kept me going. Paula is the only woman I have ever asked Linda if I could keep if she followed me home. Linda listened to what I had to say about Paula, thought about it a minute, and said, well, okay, if she would do a little cleaning and cooking. Paula is that impressive. Moreover, I am lucky enough that she is the editor of this book. You're a prize, Paula. Thank you.

Lee Klancher, editor-in-chief at MBI Publishing Company and moving force behind this book, is a good friend and a good editor, even when times have been tough—and that's not often the case between a writer and an editor. The support of Verne Holoubek and Dick Day has been a major force in my writing over the past few years; you can't believe how important it is to a writer not only to have fans out there, but fans like Verne and Dick who don't just read my words and say, yeah, okay, they're terrific. Thing is, Verne and Dick (and Paula, Dave, and Lee) have made it clear that just as readers, before meeting me, they believed in what I was saying and doing. That is not only encouraging, but the fuel that keeps me going and the reins that keep me going straight. They have put clothes on my back, tools in my hands, rest in my soul. Thank you, dear friends.

Same with the ladies on my shop calendars, especially the one I got from Gary Ummel over at the Grand Island Tree Service, especially Miss August, the incredibly fetching Tiffany. Gary, you got great taste in calendars, and Tiffany, you got great—well, Tiffany, you've brought a lot of cheer and hope into my life. August was a tough month but you made it a joy. I know by the way you look into my eyes exactly what you are thinking, you naughty girl!

INTRODUCTION

Remember what Shakespeare said about romance.
No, wait a minute. It was Sherman, and he said it about war.
—ANONYMOUS MALE

O kay, let's get this chauvinism thing on the table and settled before the first cards are dealt: I am an accomplished and experienced male chauvinist sexist pig. This book is for men only, and that's it. You can call me names if you want (bet you can't think of a new one) and you can take me to court, but if you're a woman and you read past this point {*}, I'm not going to be responsible for the consequences.

My first tractor book was *Old Tractors and the Men Who Love Them* (MBI Publishing Company, Osceola, Wisconsin, 1997) and it was made darn clear to me within moments of publication, while the ink was still warm and wet, that I had committed a major error in gender etiquette. There are women, I was told, who also love old tractors. And there are. So I apologized. Only to find out later that the selfsame women who protested my lack of diplomacy and narrow male view of things were buying the book specifically out of a prurient interest, lustily attracted to the inadvertently—but apparently irresistibly—undone side buttons on my overalls in the cover photograph. (I also learned that bookstore clerks were shelving the book among the romances because they mistakenly thought that was Fabio draped over the radiator of the Allis-Chalmers WC!)

Later I wrote a book titled *Diggin' In and Piggin' Out* (Harper Collins; New York, 1997), where I tried to make it as clear as I could that the book was meant for men. The publisher in that case would not print the gender requirement on the cover, however—something to do with the Constitution—and as a result, information about the most intimate details of the male psyche fell directly into the hands of women who probably used it in ways I don't even want to think about.

For example, in that book I revealed that, contrary to the female notion that frilly and silky things like Victoria's Secret underwear drive men crazy, it is actually mashed potatoes that do the trick. I have since heard three reports, one even in Nebraska, where women who illegally bought the book and, unrestrained by natural and international rules of romance, have combined Victoria's Secret underwear with mashed potatoes, resulting in a kind of Cupid's neutron bomb, rendering unsuspecting males utterly incapable of defending themselves in matters of the heart.

I hold myself responsible. I don't want that kind of thing to happen again. So, this book is restricted, *for male eyes only*.

This is not unfair. Far from it. Actually, I am only balancing the scales once again. Up until now it is women who have held the clear advantage, in large part unfairly gained. This book is only an honest, open, and legal way to even the field. I am astonished how many men I encounter who do not know about Woman School. Boys, there is such a thing as Woman School. You're an idiot if you think it is just a coincidence that all women do exactly the same things, say exactly the same things, demand exactly the same things, complain about exactly the same things, and uh, offer exactly the same things, if you catch my drift there on the last item. Mothers and daughters, old and young, far and wide. They're all alike because they've all gone to Woman School.

Don't bother to ask the women in your life about Woman School. They will either categorically deny there is such a thing or smile a peculiar kind of what-idiots-you-men-are smile. There is a school of thought in the art world, in fact, that just before Leonardo da Vinci painted the Mona Lisa, he asked her, "Do you-a know anything-a about-a disa Woman School-a, Mona?"

> *If you want to read about love and marriage, you've got to buy two separate books.*
> —ALAN KING

I know what you're thinking: If there is such a thing as Woman School, when do women go there? Where is it? Why don't we notice that they are gone when they go to Woman School? It's all around you, every day. That's what they do when they all go together to the "ladies room" at the same time. Do you actually believe it takes women that long to pee?! Get serious! They're in there holding a seminar on "Confusing the Idiots" or "Giving Driving Directions from the Passenger Seat" or "Packing a Purse" or "Unreasonable Demands," that's what they're doing.

Walk into a crowded ladies room sometime and see what happens. Do you think they're getting that excited because you caught them putting on lipstick or cleaning their glasses? No, your unexpected appearance in that inner sanctum threatens the security and secrecy of Woman School.

I should perhaps note here that this may not be something you want to bring up in mixed company since many women carry their denial of the existence of Woman School right up to the thin line between insistence and violence. Once up at Eric's Tavern I was outlining these contentions about there being a Woman School for a bunch of buddies, all of whom I might add were banging their chins repeatedly on the bar in their enthusiastic nods of agreement.

Just as I finished up and revealed my inside information about this issue, Patty Stoeger, who had been uncharacteristically quiet up to this point in a booth pretty much out of sight of the main seminar, then muttered loud enough for all of us to hear, "I guess that means you guys must have all gone to Asshole School."

This slim volume is an effort to correct the imbalance, to create a kind of Man School, as it were, no matter what insensitive women like Patty Stoeger might call it. Women will hate this book, not because they are excluded, not because it is crude and insensitive, but because it challenges the exclusivity of gender training.

So, fair warning, gents: If you don't want this book to disappear mysteriously, hide it under the seat of your pickup truck. Tuck it back behind something sharp and dirty in your shop. Disguise it with a dust cover from a book by Dr. Laura or Danielle Steele. Put it someplace where the woman/women in your life will never see it—tape it under the toilet seat. Disguise it as a car that is way overdue for an oil change. Keep it under the cover of your barbecue grill; she'll never see it there. Am I serious? Boys, listen up close. My wife, Linda, has not read this book. As my pal Eric says, "I may have been born on a Saturday, but it wasn't last Saturday."

WISE IN THE WAYS

So, why not a book just about love, romance, and women? What's the deal with tractors? Thing is, it is generally a good idea for writers to write what they know about, but not what they know too much about. Have you ever read an encyclopedia? Of course not. Guys who write encyclopedias know too much. You don't want to know everything when you read a book; you just want to know something. A friend of mine once asked a lawyer to write a document for him and the lawyer told him the charge would be $4 a word. My friend thought the situation over and said, okay, but he would only pay him $4 for words he didn't already know himself. In other words, four-dollar words.

My problem is that you already know a lot about women, love, and romance, probably even a lot about tractors. Maybe even more than I do. About tractors, anyway. But I'm not like the lawyer. Linda and I were once up at the local tavern talking with my two buddies, Woodrow, a plumber, and Lunchbox, an auto body repairman. I mentioned that I was writing something for *Esquire* magazine. My pals wondered how I get paid for writing something like that. I said, well, sometimes I'm paid so much for an article, agreed on beforehand; sometimes I'm paid by the word; a couple of dollars or 50 cents or whatever per word.

"You mean," said Lunchbox, "every time you write 'the' they give you $2?"

"Yeah," I said. "That's the way it works."

While the boys were still reeling from the information that I am sometimes paid for writing words even they know, Linda, sensing their confusion, leaped to my rescue. "He gets paid for using the same words over and over," she explained, "but he has to put them in different order every time."

So, here they are. Same words, different order. I am not suggesting, by combining them between the same covers, that women and tractors, romance and restoration, are alike. No, tractors and restoration are much easier, more gratifying, more fun, cheaper, quieter, easier to get along with, and something you can do with your buddies on weekends. Nor do I mean to imply that I know as much about one as the other, but I do have a pretty good idea of what I don't know about all of the above.

Old Tractors and the Men Who Love Them plucked a string on America's psychological banjo, all right. Men and women from all over the country wrote me, sent me tractor signs and parts bags and chocolate-chip cookies, telling me stories about how their fathers had loved an old tractor, about how they have an old tractor they hope to get going one of these days, how pissed they are that their granddad let his old machines go up for sale at an auction instead of leaving them to the grandkids in the will.

For one thing, I was writing about something pretty fundamental—old machines (not me, the tractors). Second, I was speaking from my heart and not my brain, and finally, I used plain English and none of that high-falutin' technical crapola. What people are saying to me is not that they learned a lot of new stuff from *Old Tractors* or *Busted Knuckles*, but that I told them what they already knew. They weren't excited about acquiring new information; they were relieved to find out they aren't the only doofuses (or maybe the word is "doofi") in the world of rusty machinery.

That's the way it is with me and sex and romance too. If you want to find out something new, check out a copy of the *Kama Sutra*. We still don't understand the old stuff, yet we should try to figure out something new. After all, isn't the most common gender-based stand-up comedy routine still the one about men leaving the toilet seat up and women being boiled about that? Why is that still funny? Because everyone is still deeply involved in the toilet seat up/toilet seat down wars, that's why.

Women, probably for all the remaining time until the world collapses into a frozen wad of ice, slag, and disposable baby diapers, will snarl about how inconsiderate it is for a man to leave a toilet lid up when he's done using it; up until pretty much the same moment, all men will remain utterly baffled. Only women get angry about this. Men just don't understand why it's such a big deal to check a toilet seat before you sit down on it. How can a woman be so fussy about whose lap she sits on and so careless about dipping the same equipment into a toilet bowl?

A female friend, Cheryl, has offered the only reasonable explanation of this curious insistence on Lid Up I have ever heard: She says it's a matter of approach. Driving down the highway at 60 miles an hour is one thing, she explains, but backing up to park is done with considerably more care, because there is considerably greater chance for mishap. Not bad, but still, why not just look at the blasted thing when you come in the door, Cheryl?

THE MAGNETO PRINCIPLE

Certainly one thing women and tractors have in common is whatever it is that makes magnetos work. When they work. Thing is, no one knows what makes magnetos work. Some people will say they know, but they don't. Ask one of these smart alecks. He will talk to you about magnetic fields and volts and amps. Ask him to show you a magnetic field or a volt or an amp. He's never seen one. He just knows they're there. Uh-huh. Remember when your brother-in-law said "Trust me on this one"? Remember how that turned out? Same with magnetic fields, volts, and amps.

Just a few days ago, Woodrow and Lunchbox and I were trying to reinstall a magneto on an Allis-Chalmers WC tractor and time it. Like many things mechanical, it was designed in just such a way by a team of master designers, trained engineers, and experienced mechanics so it can't be done. You have to line up a bunch of stuff you can hardly see, maneuver it into an almost impossible position, slide it impossibly forward, mesh it with totally hidden gears—all without the delicately balanced rotor, wheels, cams, and gears moving a fraction of an inch.

Cannot be done.

Finally, after a dozen futile tries, dripping with sweat and blood, we stood there defeated. We were still one or two gear teeth off. Lunchbox, as if inspired and suddenly enlivened, leaped at the engine, jerked the spark plug wires out of the distributor, and stuffed them back—but not into the right holes. Each was one hole out of order; the #1 wire in the #2 hole, the #2 wire in the #3 hole, and so on. "Crank it," he ordered. We did. It ran like a charm. Just like that. (Well, at least until the engine seized up because I had installed the rod caps wrong.)

"What made you think that would work?" I asked Lunchbox, utterly dazzled by his ingenuity.

"I didn't think it would work," he said. "I just did it."

Same with women.

But I've been around. I've been married now for 35 years. Two different women. (Anyone who's only been married to one woman doesn't have much of an imagination, in my opinion.) I have a mess of daughters. My mother was a woman. I don't think any of the stuff in the following pages will work, with either women or tractors. Let's be honest: What you're doing now, with either your tractor or your woman, isn't working either, right? So why not try something different?

If you try any of the techniques suggested in the following pages and your significant other (does that make us the insignificant other?) asks something like "Where are you getting these goofy ideas?" why don't you just leave me out of it? I'm trying to help you here, and if it doesn't work, well, you gotta give me some credit for trying.

I have tried to throw in just enough tractor information and shop techniques so you can pass this book off as a tech book or shop guide. Just show She Who Must Be Obeyed that it's a new book from, uh, MBI Publishing, and there's, er, this information about how to break loose stuck bolts, and, ummm, what you just learned here on this page saved the household more than the book cost, including tax and shipping.

If worse comes to worst, you can ask incredulously, "What do think? I'm learning about women, sex, and romance from a tractor book?! Hahahahahahahahahahahahahahaha. Hahahaha. Haha Ha." And then go back to reading just as quickly as you can before she can look you in the eye and see that you're lying like a dog. They can do that, you know. They learn it in Woman School. (Further techniques for disguising the subversive activity inherent in reading this book can be found in chapter 10.)

Same with the tractor stuff. Don't come whining to me if you wind up ruining an engine by following my advice. I can tell you right up front, I don't know anything about mechanics, or tractors, or engines, or transmissions, or tools, or Cindy Crawford, or tolerances, or foot-pounds, or volts. So why am I writing this book? Precisely for the reason I cited before: Guys who know everything and write books wind up with pretty boring stuff. And they make you feel like an idiot. Why, they seem to be asking, have I managed to learn all this stuff and you still don't know anything?

You won't get that from me. On almost every page you'll be able to look up and think, "You know, this guy is an idiot. I know better than that. How can a guy get to be 63 years old, a professor and author, and still not know that what he's saying here is pure and simple baloney?" And notice how much better you feel.

My old pal John Carter and I have discussed this literary issue at length. Sometimes I've even remember the next morning what it was we were talking about. For one thing, how many things can we really know about in our lives? Look around a library. Check a book catalog. Some people write books for this publisher, MBI Publishing, on carburetors, or Ford trucks, or Allis-Chalmers tractors. That's what they know about, so that's what they write about. But once they've written about the one or two things they know about, well, it's back to flipping burgers because their writing days are over.

I like to think that I came up with the idea, first applied in *Old Tractors and the Men Who Love Them*, of writing out of total ignorance. I didn't lord it over my readers by telling them the right way to do something. No, I told them how I do it—and how much it costs to repair the damage.

As John pointed out, this opens a world of writing possibilities. Like most people, I know about only one or two things, but I don't know about thousands of things. For example, I don't know about breeding fish worms, or baked Alaska, or plastic surgery, or Ulan Bator, or . . . well, obviously the list is endless. It's enough to keep me busy writing for decades.

But before you think me too wrong and too foolish as you read along, I think you will also find on almost every page that you have another reaction: "Hey, I don't know that about women and romance or tractors and tools either!" And perhaps you'll find comfort in that. Or maybe not. I have tried to mix my stated concerns and subjects carefully throughout the book so that about the time you get bored with a long passage about women and sex and stuff like that, you will find yourself moving easily and unobtrusively into a paragraph about something really exciting like a neat new ChannelLock pliers tool, or a new use for Liquid Wrench, or something else really dumb that Woodrow or Lunchbox has done.

FACE IT, WE'RE CLUELESS

Is there really a need for an operator's manual for the Model 2001 High-Maintenance Low-Mileage Woman? I'm pretty sure there is. My impression is that, far from being sophisticated about women like I am, most men haven't a clue, and if they are anywhere close to a clue, they have no idea how to put what they know into action or words.

Let me give you an example:

A couple of years ago I got a letter with the following paragraph in it from a young man about to get married. I wasn't surprised by his plan; he had already shared with me his concerns about the looming marriage. I tried in vain to explain to him then why a woman truly does hope for more preparation for The Big Day than a

> *Make love, not war. Ah, what the hell—get married and do both.*
> **—ANONYMOUS MALE**

hog in the fire pit, ice on the keg, and a large, open field. I almost had to wrestle him to the ground to convince him it might not be acceptable to the bride that he planned to have his best man and ushers dressed in blaze orange so they wouldn't waste any time getting into the field, his fiancée's mother having irresponsibly set the wedding date for the opening day of deer hunting season.

Read this excerpt from his letter to me and you'll understand why I've decided to write this book, and why this book is so important:

I'm pleased to say I've located what I think will be the perfect romantic getaway for R and me this evening. There is a monster truck rally at the Metrodome. I found a package deal that includes two tickets on the lower level, four "Super Stomper" monster bratwursts with sauerkraut and pickles, two bags of pork rinds, ten 48-ounce glasses of Old Milwaukee, and two filter masks (the exhaust fumes get pretty thick on the lower level). I told her I had something special planned, but it's otherwise going to be a complete surprise. Oh, and I rented a room from Fast Melvin's Motel. I reserved a room for an hour (optimistically) and dropped the extra $3 for sheets. Whaddya think?

This book is for that guy and the rest of you who think pretty much like he does, which is to say, all of you.

Oh Yeah, Tractors

So where am I with tractors? For those of you who've missed the last two books, *Old Tractors and the Men Who Love Them* and *Busted Tractors and Rusty Knuckles*, in those two lofty tomes I explored my new love affair with old tractors, especially Allis-Chalmers WCs. Up until seven or eight years ago, I outlined there, I'd never so much as changed the oil in a car. I just didn't like the whole notion of tinkering. I'd had this old Allis WC sitting around here for 15 years, but as long as she ran, I asked nothing more about her workings.

And she always ran. Oh, some mechanical thoughts crossed my mind now and again, like how many times have those pistons gone up and down in that old girl, precisely my own age? Why does she start when nothing else will—man, beast, or internal combustion engine? Why am I so ambivalent about motor vehicles in general, but actually quite fond of her? Why do I call my car "it" and my old Allis WC "she"?

Well, then the bug bit me, and it bit me hard one day when I was no more than working at getting a stuck oil pan plug loose. Who knows what it was that kicked over my impulse, to use a tractor metaphor, but it sure did. And then I reworked a brake, and then I got another WC, and then another, and then I built a shop, and then I bought more tools and more tools and more tools and more tractors and more tools, and pretty soon Linda gave up protesting.

Busted Knuckles tells the story of one particular tractor, a gift from an old salvage yard buddy, a wreck so utterly wretched I was challenged . . . dared . . . defied to get that piece of junk up and running. It took me two years and a heart attack, but I did it.

I'm still doing pretty much the same thing as before: taking wrecked Allises with stuck engines, spending years lovingly dismantling them, breaking everything loose, cleaning, repairing, occasionally replacing, getting them running, and driving them triumphantly to town for a recommissioning party at the town tavern. Parties complete with cheap champagne and toasts, admiring inspections by real mechanics, laughter, kidding, and more advice, all shouted over the unmuffled but cosmically significant roar of the rebuilt engine.

I suspect my grasp, as it were, of women is as primitive and bungling as my understanding of tractors. For better or worse, here it is.

When all is read and done, I hope you enjoy the book. As far as I know, it is the only book ever published that deals with love, romance, sex, marriage, women, and tractors—a literary lapse that is hard to explain. As you read about tractors and women, know that I am writing about both with love in my heart. Can't live with 'em, as they say—can't live with 'em. (Yeah, I know some people say "Can't live with 'em, can't live without 'em," but you'd be a damn fool to believe something like that. Neither is true. Norm of *Cheers* probably said it best: "Women . . . can't live with 'em . . . uh, pass the beer nuts.")

CHAPTER 1

HUNKS OF OLD IRON

*It is a truth universally acknowledged, that a single man
in possession of a good fortune must be in want of a wife.*
**—JANE AUSTEN,
*PRIDE AND PREJUDICE***

Who are you? I think that's a fair question because
it is certainly an interesting question. Of course
you are male. Not because only men love, collect, or work on old tractors, but because only men are
allowed by prior contract with the publisher to read this
book. But other than that, so far as I can tell, you could be
damn near anyone. That is the remarkable thing about
those of us who love old tractors: We can be anyone.
Absolutely anyone.

Take Doc Lawton, for instance, the good guy who has
done more fooling around with my body than anyone but
some special and selected ladies throughout my life. He works
on his old tractor when he isn't fixing up some old dog like
me. The guy who sold me my computer, Dick Day, restores
old Allises and John Deeres when he's not hustling bits,
bytes, modems, and zip drives. I got the T-shirt I'm wearing
directly from the manufacturer, Verne Holoubek, who makes
all the Harley T-shirts in the world that aren't counterfeits.

Verne collects and restores old tractors. Verne goes further than anyone I know with the notion. He actually farms with his old machinery. Then there's my father-in-law, Jake, a retired factory worker who grew up a farm boy. He loves his old John Deere B.

I pretty much make my living as a banquet speaker, which also goes a long way toward explaining my, uh, generous physique. I supplement my usual fees sometimes, when it is appropriate, by offering some of my books for sale. (And autographing them. I explain that if I autograph one of my books, it is instantly worth a dollar more to the owner. If I sign it, say, Ernest Hemingway, well, it could be worth a lot more.)

I have to give some thought to this side of the event before I schlep a 60-pound suitcase of books a quarter-mile to some hotel banquet room. Let's see, a national convention of county extension agents. They don't have a lot of money, but they'll love my books on old tractors and rural life and maybe even my book on men's food ways. So I throw an assortment of those books into my suitcase for that program. A bunch of English and history teachers—okay, my book on sod houses and the one on Willa Cather's use of food ways in her Plains fiction. And since it's only two months until Christmas, maybe my children's book and a couple of general interest books too.

Imagine this real scenario: I was about to do a program in Kansas City for a small group. They were telecommunications officers in state governments across the country. I already know these are really nice people because I met some of them at a regional meeting a few years ago. But what do you suppose they would want to read? As it turned out, the decision was accidentally made for me.

I was doing three programs in a row. First it was for some

agriculture teachers in Des Moines, who bought a pretty good hunk of the books I took with me, then those extension folks in Omaha, and they pretty well emptied out the two suitcases I'd brought. Well, darn, that left me with a fairly limited inventory in the trunk of my car. In fact, all I had left was a generous supply of my three tractor books.

Well, great. What are the chances of fairly high-placed government officials who work with high tech electronics being interested in old tractors? At the time I wrestled with whether I should even bother hauling the box into the banquet room. But what did I have to lose? I took them along and mentioned somewhere toward the end of my hilarious, inspirational, literary speech that I had some tractor books with me, and if anyone was interested they could come up and talk with me about them after the awards ceremony.

> *Good night, Irene, good night,*
> *Irene I gets you in my dreams.*
> —HUDDY LEDBETTER,
> ORIGINAL AND REAL WORDS
> TO THE SONG FREQUENTLY
> SUNG AROUND CAMPFIRES
> BY GIRL SCOUTS

I shoulda knowed. I was mobbed. The first lesson of this experience was what I was saying before: You just can't tell who is going to be an old tractor enthusiast. I thought about it a little longer and figured, well, maybe you can kinda tell who is going to be a tractor enthusiast. Al Schmitt is the mechanic up here in town; he's not an old tractor enthusiast. Kenny Lauritsen farms just down the road and around the corner from us; he isn't an old tractor enthusiast.

That makes sense, though, right? These guys work with tractors and old engines and broken parts and stuck things all day, every day. Why would they want to do that when they have some time to relax, to get away from precisely what they deal with all day, every day? Same with all those communications, medical, factory, and computer people. When they want something to do that has nothing whatsoever to do with their normal, daytime work, they look for something as far away from that work as possible. What could be further away from high-tech, modern, human-based work than a quiet shop full of shiny tools and an old tractor to work on?

Now, this has some interesting implications, especially when the time comes when you have to explain this whole old-tractor thing to other people—like the ones up at the house, if you catch my drift. The dumbest thing in the world you can do is try to come up with superficially practical reasons: economy, preservation of historical artifacts, to write a book, that kind of thing. The real reason we love old tractors, and the reason people will understand best, especially difficult (which is to say, *female*) people, is that this is therapy. It is worth doing because it will help you live happier and longer, and you can pass a lie detector test on that one.

> *People who like this sort of thing will find this the sort of thing they like.*
> —BOOK REVIEW BY ABRAHAM LINCOLN

If you want to try a remarkable exercise in sociology sometime, go to an antique tractor show. There is bound to be one close to you. *Antique Power* magazine, a darn good publication even if they do print letters from cranks, publishes an annual supplement titled *The Show Guide: Your Guide to Tractor Shows*. This publication alone is worth the price of the subscription (which at this writing is $25 a year, P.O. Box 500, Missouri City, TX 77459-9881). My favorite shows are close to my place in central Nebraska, like the Old Trusty Show at Fairmont, usually in mid-September, and the Camp Creek Threshing Show, near Waverly, in mid-July.

Good ol' Dave Mowitz started and works like a dog for an every-other-year-when-possible extravaganza just north of

Des Moines and has forced me to attend his favorite swap meet, occasionally a swamp meet, at Waukee, just west of Des Moines. All these shows are wonderful experiences, with terrific examples of restoration and tractor history, a super place to find publications, parts, information, even whole tractors. You'll find good food, wonderful people, and during my last visit to Waukee, I chatted with a young lady in overalls who made the whole trip worthwhile (there is nothing like a woman in overalls).

BUNCHA BIG LUGS

I have bought and sold all kinds of things at these meets and I will bring up the topic again: I am convinced that the reason Dave Mowitz goes to these gatherings, and it's a darn good reason, is because of the people. For one thing, they are about the nicest people you'll ever meet. I can count on one hand the unpleasant people I have encountered in my tractor work over a period of almost 10 years now. A guy I bought an Allis G from (you'll get the whole story later), and the snarly editor of a John Deere magazine (and anyone who's dealt with this jerk will know exactly who I mean), an industrial-grade ass who was eventually exiled from the ATIS web site for his uncontrollable nastiness.

And uh . . . uh . . . uh . . . you know, those are the only three I can think of. I can't believe there are any other hobbies, occupations, gatherings, or covens in which you find that sort of proportion of pleasant-to-obnoxious folks.

The first time I went to Dave's show north of Des Moines, near the village of Ankeny, he was trying to do the impossible. I can still remember my utter astonishment when I talked with him one year in January about his idea for this gigantic, world-class tractor show he wanted to put together. He went on and on about his plans, which were about as ambitious as putting on a World's Fair single-handedly.

"So," I asked, "when are you planning to throw this party? Five, six years from now?"

"No," he said. "July."

"THIS JULY? ARE YOU OUT OF YOUR MIND, MAN?!"

No, Dave meant the July coming up in about six months. And know what? The little rascal did it. The biggest blasted tractor show I've ever seen. Cars, trailers, and trucks were backed up on the interstate for miles. Announcements for traffic control were broadcast over a closed FM station so people approaching Des Moines could make appropriate plans! It was incredible.

But Dave didn't do it alone, actually. When I got there the day before this blowout was supposed to start, the place was still pretty much a shambles; acres of half-built shelters, half-erected tents, half-finished facilities, half-done everything. When I talked with Dave, however, he seemed fairly calm about it all, and then I saw his secret weapon: tractor people. His mobile phone would ring and he would say, "Uh-huh, yeah, you need that big tent up for the Allis people? I'll get someone over there right away."

About that time a clutch of good ol' boys came drifting along, wearing International, or Oliver, or Allis, or Deere caps and jackets and Dave would wave them down and say something like, "Hey, guys, how would you feel about taking a tractor over there by the Allis exhibit and helping those folks put up their tent?" In minutes the tent was up.

Actually, that isn't what usually happened. Usually he didn't have to wave anyone down. People were constantly drifting up to him, with about the same frequency as people were calling for help, offering to do whatever needed to be done.

Forget tractors. It was like a rural Woodstock. Just a bunch of good-hearted people having a good time together. It was downright inspirational. I would therefore say, if you were to ask me if you're the kind of person who might enjoy working with old tractors, "What kind of person are you? A nice guy? You might enjoy working with old tractors, then."

There is another curious conclusion to be reached from all this: The person most likely to be found collecting, working with, and enjoying old tractors is not likely to be a mechanic. At least not by vocation. We are all by consequence mechanics, because that's the language we talk and mechanics is what we inevitably wind up doing. Me? I never so much as changed the oil in a car before I got seriously interested in working on old tractors. Still haven't. Working on a car is a job; working on an old tractor is recreation.

CHAPTER 2

TOOLS AND MATRIMONY

Men have become tools of their tools.

—HENRY DAVID THOREAU

Nothing demonstrates the immense communications gap between the sexes more clearly than the respective understandings of what tools are. I cannot possibly remember the number of times Linda has said to me, or that bewildered buddies have reported to me that their wives have said to them, "What do you need more tools for?" Now, there are sometimes adjuncts to that: "Don't you have enough already?" "You haven't even used all the tools you already have!" "What do you need new tools for?" But the main thrust of the confusion is in that primary question: "What do you need more tools for?"

I'm not sure there is an answer to that question. Most men are just as baffled when confronted with that eternal question. You don't need a reason or a real need to get more tools. You get tools because they're tools, right? And they feel good. And you might need one of those, although that really doesn't matter.

And one of each tool is not enough. You need two wrenches to tighten an unanchored bolt and nut, for example. And what happens if you can't find your 9/16ths combination wrench? You can't just forget the job. So, you really need a backup 9/16ths combination wrench. Or, actually, if you are going to tighten an unanchored bolt and nut and you can't find one of your 9/16ths combination wrenches, you need three.

Actually, not even three is enough. I can't think of all the reasons, but the bottom line is, you need as many 9/16ths combination wrenches as you can get. There's no such thing as too many.

On a more serious note, some of the most prized tools in my shop cost me nothing; they were gifts. The most precious are tools I rarely even use. My dad always had a tool bench, something of a shrine for me. Partially because it was always immaculate and orderly. At one point Dad had a little black silhouette painted behind each tool so he knew exactly where it went when he was done with it.

Or what was missing when I borrowed something. I didn't do that often. He has always been pretty stuffy about my ingenuity with tools; using a wood chisel as a screwdriver, for example, or a screwdriver as a wood chisel. His tools also had a nasty habit of waiting until I was using them to break or get lost. He always noticed that (it was hard not to, with those damn silhouettes!) and he always blamed me.

A time came, however, when Mom and Dad left the old homestead and moved to a retirement home. Dad hadn't done much by way of repair work at his bench for a long time, and there's not much for the individual handyman to do at a retirement home where they have a full-time, professional repairman. Dad assembled and took along a set of tools anyway, just in case. But a moment came when we were helping the folks move when he turned to me, made a grand gesture across his tool bench with the back of his hand, and said, "Well, Rog, help yourself."

It wasn't as much fun as I thought it would be. In fact, it was sad. In fact, I cried most of the time I was taking those tools down from the wall and putting them in a box to bring to my shop. And I cried again as I unloaded them and integrated them into my own tools. As I said, I don't often use those tools (they're good tools—lots of Craftsman stuff), but when I put them on the pegs on my shop wall, I put them behind all my own, newer tools. Maybe I was thinking they are retired too. Maybe I was thinking they still had that nasty habit of breaking and getting lost. Maybe they were too important to be used.

Tools, Women, and Subterfuge

Speaking of gift tools, my daughter Joyce was once visiting us when I came in from the shop where I was taking the valves off a tractor engine head. I was using a screwdriver to pry down on the valve spring, then trying gingerly to pull the valve keepers out with longnose pliers, then easing up slowly on the screwdriver to release the pressure on the spring. If you have ever used this stupid technique yourself, then you almost certainly have a round scar in the middle of your forehead, about an inch across, where that spring slid out from under the screwdriver and fired with the velocity of a rifle bullet right into your forehead. You know, pretty much in the same place where the champagne cork hit you when you were leaning over a bottle and trying to pry the cork loose last New Year's Eve.

Anyway, when daughter Joyce saw that blemish on my otherwise perfect façade, she said something like, "Isn't there a tool for that kind of job so you don't keep getting hit in the head?" (I can't remember if she was at our place one of the other times a valve spring hit me in the head, or whether Linda had shared that information with her another time. Women think that's pretty funny, you getting hit in the head by a valve spring.)

Joyce wasn't married, and she must not have been dating Andrew because he's a tool guy and she would have known (probably would have learned it in Woman School) that a woman never suggests to a man that he might perhaps want to buy a tool. Because he is going to buy that tool. And a couple more. Linda quickly jumped in on the conversation, she being a full professor with tenure at Woman School. "If there is such a thing, and if you need one [author's note: haha-hahahahahahahahaha. "If you need one . . . !" Hahahahaha-hahahahaha!], maybe we can get it for you while we're in town tweaking up the credit card limit this afternoon."

Well, I'm not exactly new at this either. "Okay," I countered. "Here it is, in this Sears catalog. It's the only place in the world where they sell valve spring compressors, and man, this price is the lowest I've seen in, well, almost 30 years. What luck!"

Linda knew better, of course. She knew there are other places to get a valve spring compressor tool, and she knows there are cheaper models. "Didn't I see a valve spring com-pressor tool in the last J. C. Whitney catalog? And wasn't it about half this price?"

"Uh, maybe, but I think that was an electric motor valve spring compressor tool, and all my Allises are internal combustion."

The trick here is to hold your gaze. Don't blink. Look right straight at her. It won't be easy, but if you break and look away, or run, she's going to figure out what's going on and then say something like, "You've gotten along pretty well with the screwdriver so far; next time one of those Subcontinent-Subquality Tools catalogs comes in, I'll look through it and get you one for Christmas."

This is a very bad turn of events. You don't want this to happen. When Linda buys me tools, they are those Saladmaster tools you get through television ads: "Chops cabbage, slices radishes, purees avocados, loosens stuck manifold studs!" You don't want that.

But I do owe an apology here to Precious Moments, as I call her when I smell the possibility of passing tool purchase across . . . or under . . . the requisition desk. Last Father's Day I decided I wanted . . . uh, needed a new compressor. I started early, about Valentine's Day, with a note enclosed

> *YOUR WIFE JUST CALLED, SHE SAID TO BUY ANYTHING YOU WANT.*
> —SIGN BEHIND CUSTOMER SERVICE DESK, CABELA'S SPORTING GOODS STORE, KEARNEY, NEBRASKA

with the chocolates. She asked what a compressor does and, thinking fast, I told her it is primarily a safety device that would almost pay for itself by reducing our expenditures for Band-Aids and disinfectant—maybe a couple of thousand dollars per annum.

I showed it to her in the catalog, and this is really important so memorize it before your wife throws away this book: Patronize tool catalogs that offer nothing whatsoever by way of scale in their photographs of the tools. I mean, hey, this 90-gallon, two-cycle, 15-horsepower compressor is only 2 1/2 inches high in the catalog. It looks perfectly harmless. A little pricey, but safety is never really too expensive. Then I told her there are a lot of details that she'd need to be really sure about, and if she got the wrong one, it would have to go back, and maybe even go back again, until we got one that suited my "needs."

She went for it. She said, "Why don't you go ahead and order it over the phone and I'll pick it up when I go to town next week?" So, she didn't hear the guy at the other end assure me that they would have a loader to put this black, hulking monster into her truck, and that they'd tie it down so it wouldn't fall out and kill innocent bystanders, and that I'd need a loader to move this brute when she got it here.

"Fine," I said into the phone, smiling in Linda's direction. "No problem. My wife will pick it up."

When she drove into our yard, the front wheels on her truck only touching the ground often enough so she could get some steering, I demonstrated amazement that she didn't understand what the size of this thing was going to be, and that I'd of course have to build on an addition to the shop for it, and that, gosh, I sure will be more careful to find out in advance about the size of any future tool purchase way before I send her to pick it up.

Yeah. Right.

THE HIDDEN COSTS OF TOOLS

My buddy Woodrow is at least as mystified by women as I am, but sometimes he has had insights that have hit me between the eyes like the legendary 2-by-4 that hit that mule.

He was once at my place working on a plumbing problem and he was kicking himself because we needed a new kitchen sink faucet set and, he told me, he had just attended a big plumbing convention and won a door prize he'd refused to accept—a new set of solid brass kitchen faucets.

Refused to accept? Without putting down his pipe wrench, he explained that he could see right away what that $120 set of kitchen faucets would cost him if he brought it home to Dottie. A weekend of good fishing and hunting time lost installing it, and new brass fixtures for all the other sinks in the house. New cupboard latches and handles in the kitchen. Probably a new floor, maybe a refrigerator. He calculated that those free faucets probably would have set him back nearly $1,000 if he had accepted them, and then he condensed this idea in that wonderful poetry I love so much about the rural American countryside. "Rog," he said, looking me square in the eye. "Listen to me. The most expensive gift you can ever give a woman is a tape measure."

Wow. For knowing nothing at all about women, ol' Woodrow sure knows a lot about women.

THE SCAVENGED TOOLS DIVISION

I still believe in using common household items as shop tools. They are not nearly as pretty as the ones I get from Sears, but they are a darned sight cheaper and often just as useful. For example, I use garden hose hangers for my air hoses and extension cords (not to mention that I hang those lines from my rafters. I am always puzzled by guys who let air hoses and electric lines clutter up the floor. I'm not exactly Mr. Tidy, but that seems to be asking for trouble, especially since the time I dropped some melted welding rod onto my air hose and was surprised by the blast of compressed air blowing up the leg of my overalls).

I have looked around for decent parts and hardware bins for years, but they are always too flimsy, too large, too small, too expensive, too something or other. But now I have a system that is working wonderfully for me, and it costs nothing. Good price.

For smaller parts I cut the tops off of rectangular motor oil quart containers I pick out of the garbage up at Al's automotive service in town. I like the yellow ones for bolts, nuts, washers, that kind of thing, because then I can write down with a marker what is inside. They sit nicely on the shelf, are unbreakable, and take up a minimal amount of room.

For larger items like parts, I use cat food containers (the only decent reason I can come up with for having a cat, as a matter of fact). On these I don't cut off the tops, however. I use them as is, again with a label written on the handle side of the container so I can just stick it back on the shelf, or look down the shelf and pick out whatever it is I'm looking for.

For much larger parts, like whole carburetors, magneto rotors, soldering tools, or transmission lugs, I use the larger, 2 1/2-gallon, plastic containers bulk oil comes in. With these I cut off part of the top (but not the handle part) so I can get larger parts to fit. Again, I write the contents on the side, put them side-by-side on the shelf, and still tell what's inside without peering into the dark interior. When they get shopworn, I just throw them out. The supply of motor oil, cat food, and bulk oil containers around here is endless.

I am perhaps most proud in the Scavenged Tools Division of the large, sturdy, square trays I use under engines or transmissions I'm cleaning. They are just the right size—about 2x3 feet, liquid-proof, they don't leak, they're sturdy, the sides are just the right height, and every other one has a nice handle with which to slide it around the shop floor. My mechanic friends were dazzled by this nice equipment, and even more surprised when they figured out they are halves of old hard-shell suitcases! I've done a lot of traveling and wear out suitcases every two or three years. I just take them apart at the hinges, tear out all the lining, and there they are. Perfect.

No one ever has enough hardware, nuts, bolts, washers, that kind of thing. No one. But I walk to town and back every day for mail. You'd be amazed at the hardware I pick up along the way—bolts, washers, nuts, and on a couple of occasions, even tools. My best tin snips were lying there, right in the middle of the road. I think they were God's way of saying, "You're a good boy, Rog."

TOOL BARGAINS

I have groused elsewhere about crummy tools, equipment, and supplies and quoted my old buddy Lunchbox in his admonition that the most expensive thing you can buy is a cheap tool. But there are some real bargains out there. It's not as if you have to spend a lot of money every time you find you need something. I am astonished, for example, by a wonderfully inexpensive and useful substance I have found for cleaning greasy, dirty hands. Hand cleaner.

There was a time when I used gasoline (yikes!) or kerosene for cleaning my hands, which then took on for all the world the semblance of lizard skin. But now there are dozens of really terrific hand cleaners that amaze me every time by their ability to take off just about any kind of substance I don't want on my skin, while at the same time leaving the skin there. I'd tell you my favorites, but I really don't have any favorites. I use Goop from a wall dispenser (I have one in my shop and one in the washroom over the sink) and a squirt bottle of orange stuff with grit in it on my workbench. No need for second best or improvisation here.

Sometimes I find I have better luck using a tool meant for something else rather than the tool that seems designed for the purpose. I like Vise-Grip tools (they were invented and are made right here in my home state of Nebraska, after all) and ChannelLock because someone there really knows how to name tools, e.g., Big Azz Pliers, but more and more I find I am turning to pipe wrenches for the most challenging jobs of twisting bolts and studs.

MAKING YOUR OWN TOOLS

I am just tickled as can be with my own ingenuity and talents when I actually make a tool myself. Some are fairly simple; I cut out a profile on a strip of scrap iron to make a wrench for opening the bungs of 50-gallon drums, for example.

Others are more complex. In one of my previous tractor books I mentioned that I wished I had a heating stove for my shop, so I could burn some of the substantial quantities of discarded motor and transmission oil I was accumulating. I got some letters from readers suggesting where I could find oil burners, or very complicated plans for making them, or offers from manufacturers to sell me very expensive ones. Well, gosh, I really didn't want to invest a lot of work, time, and money into this thing, and I really didn't need an industrial-grade furnace.

My shop is small, I burn wood for heat, and I'm happy with my $35 wood stove. What I really wanted was not a blast furnace but some way I could drip oil and keep a small flame going after I heated up the shop with wood, just an auxiliary fueling system. I wanted, mostly, to get rid of that old, dirty oil without just throwing it away.

My wood stove is a big old brick-lined vertical burner. It is a little inconvenient because I have to stoke it from the top and take ashes out from the bottom, but it works very well. When I start it up there's a pretty good flame, but most of the time coals just glow in the bottom, maybe a small piece of wood crackles away. The thing doesn't shudder with an internal inferno, or turn red hot, or suck tractor parts into the draft port. What I need is a small fire to maintain warmth for the shop, not a blast furnace to blow massive amounts of heat into it. Maybe if I just dripped a little oil from the top onto the little fire at the bottom . . .

I scrounged around in my can box and found a medium-sized coffee can that fit easily, but not loosely, inside another. The larger can I figured I would fasten to the wall as a holder for the smaller one. I drilled a hole in the side of the smaller can, near the bottom, and mounted a brass valve in it. I screwed the larger can to the wall, above and a few feet away from the stove, and cut a slot in the front so I could slide the smaller can, valve and all, into it. I thought this double can system would let me take it down and clean it out or repair it, for one thing, but also head off any dripping or leaking.

I attached a length of quarter-inch copper tubing to the valve, long enough not only to reach the top of the stove but also to put a generous loop in it as a kind of safety trap to make sure no flame would go back up the tubing and to the can of oil on the wall. This turned out to be an unnecessary concern since the tube never even gets warm, let alone fire-hot, but the loop is still a good idea for safety. I drilled a hole in the flat top of the stove and put the tube end into it, making sure that only the tip of it dips into the firebox so it doesn't get too hot. Since the fire grate in my stove is a good 3 feet under the tube's opening and flame rarely reaches it (never when I'm dripping oil into the fire), the tubing is cool to the touch just inches away from the stove top.

As I noted above, I start the fire with kindling, old gaskets, scrap paper from the shop, whatever I've been throwing in there when it wasn't lit. Then I stoke it with as big a piece of firewood as the top opening will take. Once the fire dies back to a nice simmer, I open the valve on the coffee can at the top of the tubing until it is just dripping on the log, which serves as a wick. This setup cuts way back on the amount of wood I burn, produces a clean fire with no noticeable smoke or smell, and keeps the shop nice and warm.

I run the oil through a screen sieve before putting it into my coffee can reservoir. And I've found that I can save even more on wood by dropping a couple of thick magazines (telephone books or thick catalogs are even better) into the bottom of the stove and letting the oil drip and soak on them as wicks. They burn away slowly in a very nice, quiet fire and don't wind up in a landfill or a dump.

I never burn oil when I'm not in the shop; in fact, I usually try to time my fueling so the reservoir on the wall is pretty much empty by the time I'm ready to close down. I find I burn a gallon or two of oil a day with this system, which also means I have to check and fill up the reservoir every hour or two. But it makes me feel so darn good that I am getting some use out of something that might otherwise find its way into the soil or water that I really don't mind the minor inconvenience at all.

STEALING . . . UH, BORROWING TOOLS

One of the hardest things for me to get used to about living in a small town (Dannebrog, Nebraska, population 324) was the notion of borrowing tools. And that is the operative expression: "borrowing tools." While people here are always borrowing tools, it never occurs to anyone to return them. When Eric Nielsen moved a few years ago, I asked him if he needed any help; he said no, that his plan was to have everyone come over and pick up their things he had borrowed. This would leave him with just a couple of cardboard boxes of his own stuff, which he could easily haul in the trunk of his car.

In fact, people here get really huffy if you make any noise at all about them not returning the snow shovel they borrowed, oh, six years ago. Woodrow and Lunchbox were looking over our plumbing once a couple of years ago; Woodrow commented on our spiffy water filter. That, he told Lunchbox, was precisely what he needed at his house, and that he should borrow mine and install it at his own home!

He was proposing not only that Lunchbox borrow an integral part of our plumbing, but that he install it in his own home. They were both astonished by my astonishment.

I should have known: For decades now Woodrow has had a canoe, but he borrows my paddles. See, I always thought that if you had a canoe, you would pretty much want to have paddles. Not Woodrow. Not here. Not if you can borrow them from someone else.

> *Man is a tool-using animal. . . . Without tools, he is nothing; with tools he is all.*
>
> —THOMAS CARLYLE
> (AUTHOR'S NOTE: I BET THIS CARLYLE GUY HAD ONE HELL OF A GOOD SHOP!)

My brother-in-law once dropped by to borrow a couple of house jacks. He was trying to level a drooping corner of his house. Well, sure. I've done that myself. You jack up the sag, put blocks, bricks, supports, and shims under it, lower the jack so the house rests on the new support, pull out the jacks, and there you are, right?

No, that is not right. I was thinking like I used to think, not like a Dannebrognagian. Steve borrowed my jacks, jacked up the house, and that was it. He walled up the foundation again and the jacks are in there apparently rusting for all eternity. Still mine, but pretty much out on permanent loan.

The bottom line here is that you don't loan out anything you may conceivably ever want to use again yourself. I can't recall ever having had anything borrowed returned. I have on occasion gone by the miscreant's house to retrieve something (an action, I have since learned, that is considered socially acceptable if a trifle inconsiderate) to find my property dismantled or broken. A borrowed tractor was once returned to me with parts broken off: "Won't take much to weld that back on," the borrower reassured me as he drove off. He was the same one who shortened a log chain by putting knots in it. Putting knots in a log chain and then putting it under strain pretty much shortens it permanently. As he drove off that time, he said, "You can cut those knots out with a cutting torch in no time."

I don't know if that is as bad, however, as the guy who scolded me for coming around to borrow my chainsaw, and scolding me for not repairing it from the last time he borrowed it. He was flabbergasted the next autumn when I wouldn't loan it to him again. He says I'm "uppity."

CHAPTER 3

RELIGION AND TRACTORS

(AND UH, OH YEAH, LOVE AND ROMANCE)

God created woman. And boredom did indeed cease from that moment—but many other things ceased as well.

—FRIEDRICH NIETZSCHE

I believe that God looks after fools and drunkards, although the vanity of that assertion does make me a bit uneasy. It's like my old friend, Dick Whitefoot, who used to throw a big Christmas feed for all of the area's "drunks, derelicts, and everyone that nobody likes." He always noted that I was thus triply honored at the occasion. And there's nowhere the protection is more needed or more generously applied than in a tractor mechanic's shop. I should have a little cross-stitch sampler hanging in my shop saying, "Whew—that was close!"

It's not as if men are tougher than women, or immune to pain. Pain is pain, qualitatively speaking. But not, and this is not only important but a fact first revealed in these pages, quantitatively. Let's say Subject A, a female human, has a cold. She kisses Subject B, a male human, so he gets the self-same germs, very same cold, very same time. Two people, two colds. One cold per person, right?

Well, yes, in a way, but that's not the way a cold works. Colds saturate our bodies, every fiber and bone, every nook and snotty cranny. Okay, the woman in question may have more nooks and crannies, and God bless 'em all, but let's face it, she weighs 122 pounds and therefore has a 122-pound cold. Male B has a 248-pound body and therefore has a 248-pound cold. Or a bit more than twice as much cold as Female Subject A.

Another useful metaphor: A honeybee crashes into your windshield. Ouch. A 747 airliner crashes into your windshield. Double ouch, right? Two flying things hit your car. Not the same results.

As for the uni-gender situation of childbirth, which women insist on bringing up whenever this conversation arises, well, uh, that's what you get for eating that apple in the Garden of Eden. Ask any Baptist.

That's one of the reasons I never feel too bad when I hurt myself in the shop. I come into the house with blood dripping from my fingertips or into my shoe tops, the smell of burning hair and flesh about me, large, black blotches on my arms, legs, and nose hairs, my clothes torn to ragged shreds. Linda says, "EEEEEEEEK! ARE YOU OKAY?!" And I say, "Yeah, why?" because I know what I could have looked like.

I have written elsewhere (a naked inducement for you to buy my other books) about the demons of the shop that make little springs and ball bearings roll under shop equipment, not to be seen again until Jesus comes to reclaim the dead. All of us who are shop mechanics will be looking for those damn springs and miss the roll call up yonder, I'm betting. There are imps and devils that make sure the stuck valve is the very last one you check. Ogres that cause leaks in oil containers and hide cockleburs in shop rags. And blue meanies that guide little beads of welding slag into the shoelace holes of your shop boots.

But not always. Sometimes the angels do come along and bestow such wonders, all faith is restored. But my cosmology (Yeah, I know, every gearhead reading this thinks I'm talking about the thick, sticky stuff you put on rifles to keep them from rusting up in the jungle. That's okay, it'll work.) tells me that the real Master Mechanic is the Native American Coyote. That critter you can never trust, the one you think has just done you bad when he has really graced you with his kindness. Or who is actually dumping on you just when you think everything is going along dandily.

Orange bright,
Like golden lamps in a green light.
—ANDREW MARVELL

Example: I was welding along gleefully one day when I distinctly smelled burning rubber. Early on in my welding career I learned to pay attention to such subtle signals. I don't know how many times I flicked up my welding mask, just pleased as punch with the long, straight, deep, even bead I had just completed (unfortunately, however, welding my Vise-Grip pliers to the welding table, but still . . .), only to find that I really should have paid closer attention to the smoke rising from under the table where a cardboard box of discarded overalls was in full blaze. When I got a whiff of this inadvertent vulcanizing, I quickly decided to do a follow-up.

Whoops. Didn't need to. Just as I started to lift my mask, another of my senses sprang into action: a faint hissing sound started, grew, exploded, and then roared. (Note: Explosions are never good in the kitchen, shop, or relationship. Write that down somewhere.) In less time than it took me to lift the welding mask, burning slag had dropped onto the air hose I'd thoughtfully arranged directly under my welding table, melted through it, and gave the compressed air the freedom it longed for.

I forget exactly what I said, but I remember quite distinctly that it was poetic and colorful. (I have always wondered if there are any minister-mechanics. What do they say when they hit their thumb with a hammer, or smash their knuckles between an engine and transmission, or pick up a red-hot bolt? Do they indeed hire professional mechanics to say the appropriate phrases for them? Do they get a dispensation from a higher authority for such occasions? You can't tell me—I'm not stupid—that they say nothing at all.) At any rate, I turned off the compressor, assessed the damage, cut off the damaged part of the hose (too close to the end to splice), and reaffixed the receptacle on the end.

> Love is such a pretty, pretty thing
> It touches the young and old;
> It's just like a plate of boarding room hash,
> And many a man has it sold . . .
> —AMERICAN FOLKSONG

I took the 2-foot piece of now useless hose and started to throw it toward the trash. Now, I know that a lot of you are like me, and a lot of you know someone like me even if you are not like me. Linda once marked on her calendar the day I threw something away. I honestly believe that absolutely everything has one more use. And then it goes into the shop stove to heat the place. And then the ashes go around the trees.

This dimension of the male psyche is not easy to explain. I boiled a ham day before yesterday. Yesterday Linda pulled out the ham and finished baking it. This morning I planned to bail out the ham water and put it in bottles, then freeze it for soup, which I love. I heat up the stock, throw in some pasta or beans, onions, ham, bacon, some celery, garlic, whatever else is handy. And I can eat for days.

I was complaining gently that since I was busy with the soup, I was going to lose a day I could have spent in the shop. Linda said sweetly, innocently, "Why don't you just throw away the ham water? Why do we need it in our freezer?"

Me. Throw away something useful. Thus denying everything from the Great Depression and World War Aye Aye and throw away nutritious ham water. Now, I ask you, just what the hell do you think was going through her mind when she said that? I know what was going through mine: "Him? Oh, why not just throw him out? He's old. He takes a lot of work. There are plenty of old farts around. Why do we need him in our freezer?"

This woman knows me better than any other human being alive, including you, and my parents, or anyone else. So why would she say something like, "Why don't you just throw away the ham water?" What's more, she said it as if she had said, oh maybe, "Do you mind if I throw out all the empty toilet paper rollers in the upstairs bathroom?" You know, something really useless.

Well, maybe that's not a good example, because actually, I've found a terrific use for empty toilet paper rollers. It's as if she said, "Is it okay if I just throw out these old walnut shells?" Well, that's not a good example either, actually, because walnut shells are real oily and make terrific starters for fireplace fires. It's as if she said she was going to throw away . . . Hmmm. Right offhand I can't think of anything so useless that I'd throw it away, but just imagine she said something real obvious about something I actually might throw away.

Anyway, there I was, standing in the shop with a shortened air hose and a 2-foot piece of useless (hahahahahahahahahaha) air hose in my hand. Next I got ready to lift the head off an engine. I lowered my lift winch, got the chains ready to attach to the rocker arm lugs to pull the head, and I thought, you know, I really should put something over those lugs to keep from buggering up the threads when I start cranking that thing up.

But what could I put over those engine lugs to protect the threads? A piece of copper tubing? A bunch of washers? Duct tape? No, all that is too clumsy. What I really need, I thought, is a sleeve of some soft substance, something that will just fit over the lug but into the chain link, something like, something like . . . this piece of air hose I have in my hand, right here.

Ol' Coyote was at work. He had me going there for a while when I burned a hole in the hose, but then he made it clear what he had in mind for me. No way I'd cut up a perfectly good air hose, but since I had this little stub of what a woman might call "useless" hose anyway, my problem was solved.

CHAPTER 4

DATING, TERRITORY, AND GOOD OL' BOSWELL FLICK

There is nothing wrong with teenagers that reasoning with them won't aggravate.

—UNKNOWN

I t's not as if Coyote is a bad guy. He just has his way of doing things and sometimes he points out little things to us about ourselves and gives us a chance to learn a little something, mostly about the real troublemakers in our lives—ourselves.

Boswell Flick told me a pretty sad story about Coyote working in his shop not long ago. Seems his daughter Peanut was about to start her dating career, what with her being 16 years old and all, and he decided that this time he was going to do things right. I understand this. For one thing, I have a 16-year-old daughter, and for another, I was once 17. This is not a good combination, a boy and a girl. A cyber-friend sent me a set of rules which, Luther-like, I nailed on daughter Antonia's bedroom door, to wit, viz:

TEN SIMPLE RULES
FOR DATING MY DAUGHTER

Rule 1: If you pull into my driveway and honk, you'd better be delivering a package, because you're sure not picking anything up.

Rule 2: You do not touch my daughter in front of me. You may glance at her, so long as you do not peer at anything below her neck. If you cannot keep your eyes or hands off of my daughter's body, I will remove them.

Rule 3: I am aware that it is considered fashionable for boys of your age to wear their trousers so loosely that they appear to be falling off their hips. Please don't take this as an insult, but you and all of your friends are complete idiots. Still, I want to be fair and open-minded about this issue, so I propose this compromise: You may come to the door with your underwear showing and your pants 10 sizes too big, and I will not object. To ensure that your clothes do not, in fact, come off during the course of your date with my daughter, however, I will take my electric nail gun and fasten your trousers securely in place to your waist.

Rule 4: I'm sure you've been told that in today's world, sex without using a "barrier method" of some kind can kill you. Let me elaborate. When it comes to sex, I am the barrier, and I will kill you.

Rule 5: It is usually understood that in order for us to get to know each other, we should talk about sports, politics, and other issues of the day. Please do not do this. The only information I require from you is an indication of when you expect to have my daughter safely back at my house, and the only word I need from you on this subject is *early*.

Rule 6: I have no doubt you are a popular fellow, with many opportunities to date other girls. This is fine with me as long as it is okay with my daughter. Otherwise, once you have gone out with my little girl, you will continue to date no one but her until she is finished with you. If you make her cry, I will make you cry.

Rule 7: As you stand in my front hallway, waiting for my daughter to appear and more than an hour goes by, do not sigh and fidget. If you want to be on time for the movie, you should not be dating. My daughter is putting on her makeup, a process that can take longer than painting the Golden Gate Bridge. Instead of just standing there, why don't you do something useful, like change the oil in my car?

Rule 8: The following places are not appropriate for a date with my daughter: places where there are beds, sofas, or anything softer than a wooden stool. Places where there are no parents, police officers, or nuns within eyesight. Places where there is darkness. Places where there is dancing, holding hands, or happiness. Places where the ambient temperature is warm enough to induce my daughter to wear shorts, tank tops, midriff T-shirts, or anything other than overalls, a sweater, and a goose down parka zipped up to her throat. Movies with a strong romantic or sexual theme are to be avoided; movies that feature chainsaws are okay. Hockey games are okay. Old folks homes are better.

Rule 9: Do not lie to me. I may appear to be a potbellied, balding, middle-aged, dimwitted has-been. But on issues relating to my daughter, I am the all-knowing, merciless god of your universe. If I ask you where you are going and with whom, you have one chance to tell me the truth, the whole truth, and nothing but the truth. I have a shotgun, a shovel, and 65 acres behind the house. Do not trifle with me.

Rule 10: Be afraid. Be very afraid. It takes very little for me to mistake the sound of your car in the driveway for a chopper coming in over a rice paddy near Hanoi. When my Agent Orange starts acting up, the voices in my head frequently tell me to clean the guns as I wait for you to bring my daughter home. As soon as you pull into the driveway, you should exit your car with both hands in plain sight. Speak the perimeter password, announce in a clear voice that you have brought my daughter home safely and early, then return to your car. There is no need for you to come inside. The camouflaged face at the window is mine.

I sympathized with Bos when he told me Peanut was about to go out on her first date, and I was ready when he drove his battered blue Ford F-150 pickup truck into our drive to report on how things had gone.

Remembering his own youth and the painful times he'd had to confront his dates' fathers, he decided that the thing to do was to inflict pretty much the same agony on HIS daughter. So he informed her that any boy who intended to take her out, alone, in a car, for more than an hour, to anything other than choir practice, was going to have to introduce himself and explain himself to the Man Himself, Boswell Flick.

Well, Peanut was not at all tickled by this notion but since it was presented as a *sine qua non* (that's Latin for "bottom line"), she knew she'd have to go along with Bos. Not being an inconsiderate father, and seeing Peanut's distress, he softened his demands by giving her some choices: She could bring her young suitor to meet ol' Bos in the house where he would be watching something on the Playboy Channel, or in his study where he would be working on his matchbook collection, or out in the shop where he would be working on a tractor.

Peanut didn't have to give this a lot of thought; since her potential date excelled in his welding class, she would bring him out to Bos' shop.

When the day of the First Date arrived, Bos made his preparations by spending all day in the shop, working on transmissions, welding, removing and replacing bull gears, wrestling engines off and on tractors. By the time the witching hour arrived, he was dirty, he was stinky, he was ugly, he was bloody, he was pissed. He was prepared. He was Bos.

EVENING FALLS ON THE SHOP

Peanut's date, Kevin Parsons, arrived in a battered, mufflerless 1987 Chevy Nova, got out of the passenger side since there wasn't any handle on the driver side, and left the engine running because he wasn't sure if it would start again if he turned it off—and he wasn't altogether certain of the kind of reception he was going to get out in Bos' shop.

Bos saw the boy drive into the yard. He turned up the ZZ Top on the stereo, cranked up the compressor to increase the noise level, and smeared a little extra gun grease on his face just in case he'd missed anything. The boy approached the shop pretty much like a stray dog edges toward a hot dog dropped on a highway. Bos turned off the right-angle grinder in his hand, threw it to the floor, blew some snot out of his nose and through the open door of the shop, and took a step toward the boy.

He held out a filthy, bloody hand—the same of the previously noted snot-blowing. The boy took it. They howdied. Bos leaned back on his tractor and made the speech he'd been rehearsing for 15 years:

"Son, I appreciate you coming around and I hope you have a pleasant and safe evening. You know Peanut. You wouldn't be here if you didn't understand that there is something about her worthy of attention. I think you can understand that I adore her, since she is my only child. And that if anyone should bring her any harm, on purpose or accidentally, I would pretty much have to kill the son-of-a-bitch, dismember him, and eat his body parts. All that I didn't feed to my dogs, anyway. All I ask is that you bring her home safe and happy and in precisely the same condition, if you catch my drift, as she is when you leave this yard.

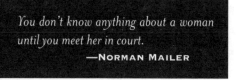

You don't know anything about a woman until you meet her in court.
—NORMAN MAILER

"I will not tolerate you drinking and driving while you have Peanut in that . . . that . . . [Boswell gestured toward the lugging and now ominously smoking car]. Frankly, you don't know shit about driving as it is, and even one beer can alter your driving abilities enough to cause an accident, and once again let me remind you, if Peanut suffers so much as a broken fingernail because you've been drinking, you better hope you never have a medical emergency and need a catheter, because they won't be able to figure out where to stuff it.

"Which is to say, no drinking and driving. Got that?"

[Bos tapped his filthy forefinger on the boy's chest four times, leaving four FBI-identifiable fingerprints on the lad's damn near new shirt.] The boy nodded.

Bos continued:

"Absolutely no drinking. And this is a Saturday night, and every other ignorant puke in this county is out there slopping down brews and driving the gravel, thinking that way he's safe from the cops. But the fact of the matter is he is endangering everyone else on the roads. You gotta drive for them too, boy. Understand? Even if you don't endanger your life and manhood by drinking, you're gonna have to drive tonight for every other goddamn idiot out there who *is* drinking and driving. Do you get that? Any drinking and driving, and you are dead meat. Even if it's some other ignorant idiot."

The boy nodded.

Bos blew his nose again and flicked some blood off a gash on the back of his left hand.

Bos looked at the boy for a good minute, then at the car, now showing every sign of doing a Mount St. Helens right there in the Flick farmyard. "Now, son, I understand your folks know me. I don't recognize the name Parsons. Where do I know your folks from?"

Kevin cleared his throat and said in a voice barely audible over the sounds of Bos' compressor and ZZ Top's "Nationwide," "Yessir. Actually, it isn't my folks. It's my grandparents. They used to run the tavern over in Limbo. I washed dishes there. I saw you there a lot of times."

Bos reached over and turned down the stereo. "The Limbo Tavern?" he asked.

"Yessir," the boy answered respectfully. "I helped you out to your car a couple of times even."

Bos said that at that point he felt a lot like that time he stepped on the rake and it put that crease in his forehead that is still there to this day. Bos said he swallowed hard and reached for his back pocket. "Here's 20 bucks, kid. Have a nice time," he said.

The boy smiled and went back to the car where Peanut was waiting, wondering if her friend would survive his interrogation.

As usual, the real question of course was whether Boswell would survive.

Yep. If there is a god, it's Coyote. And if gods hang around anywhere during their time off, it's in the shops of tractor mechanics.

CHAPTER 5

THE ROMANCE OF TRACTOR SHOPPING

The Lord giveth and the Lord taketh away.
And if that's not a square deal, I'll kiss your butt.
—GAR DONNELSON

Unless you're a tractor rustler, you pretty much eventually are going to have to face someone to acquire a tractor. It's not a pretty process. I think we can divide your basic tractor sellers into (at least) four categories: Proud Parents, Opportunists, Not a Clue, and No Nonsense.

The variety that is the most fun, in fact, a joy, are the first, Proud Parents. They are often old farmers who genuinely love their old tractor or machinery and are mostly looking for a good home for their old iron. This is always where you will get your best buy because money is, generally speaking, only a minor detail, even an inconvenience in the negotiations.

Mostly this seller will want to know what kind of provisions you have made to care for this beloved item he is about to part with: What sort of provisions have you made to shelter his child? Do you understand that it needs regular oil changes? And nothing but 10W40 Quaker State oil? Do you intend to weld up that broken lever on the torque magnifier?

If so, then let's see a sample of your welding work! And exact-ly what will be the seller's visitation rights after the purchase?

Such acquisitions are a good deal more trouble than a flat-out purchase, but they're often the most rewarding too. These are the machines that come complete with the original operator's manuals, maintenance schedules, umbrellas, spare carburetors, machinery mounting brackets, and associated tools. The machines are almost certain to have been well taken care of for a long time before they fall into your hands.

The purchase price is likely to be the most reasonable too, if you successfully pass inspection as a prospective hus-band . . . uh, owner. In fact, I have acquired a number of my Allis WCs from owners in this category as outright gifts, or in exchange for token payment. Two of the tractors in my pos-session came to me in exchange for a set of as many of my var-ious books as I could assemble in one pile.

The principal disadvantage of this kind of purchase is that the machine comes with a load of responsibility, even guilt. These may indeed be the best machines you'll get for your collection, but they also carry with them the greatest dif-ficulties. If you have a soul at all, you are also taking on all the obligations of a caretaker and guardian, not just a plain ol' ordinary owner as you might be with an outright purchase. You'll feel bad every time you leave this machine out in the weather, every time you do a sloppy job of repairing or fall behind in the prescribed maintenance schedule.

And if the time ever comes to sell this thing, you wind up having to do the same sort of screening you went through when you first acquired it. These acquisitions cannot be dumped through want ads or auctions. You gotta meet this pretender to the throne . . . uh, tractor seat. And you'll have to keep this guy's phone number and address forever because

you may have to report the tractor's whereabouts to the original parent.

On the other hand, think how proud you'll feel if and
when the owner deems you worthy of holding the crank of his
prize! It is quite literally like getting approval of a fair lady's
hand from her parents.

MAIL-ORDER BRIDES . . . UH, TRACTORS

On the other hand, the very worst people to buy tractors,
or to acquire brides from, are those who believe they have in
their possession an unparalleled treasure of which you, disgusting creature that you are, will never be worthy of. At least
not without enormous sacrifice, expenditure, and commitment on your part.

You're probably thinking I am talking money here.
Wrong-o. Money is definitely the most common element in
possible purchases from Opportunists.
(I write "possible" because I am hoping
that once you sense you are dealing with
one of these idiots, you will beat a hasty
and protracted retreat. There is no such
thing as a square deal, let alone a bar-

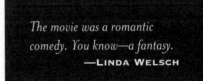

*The movie was a romantic
comedy. You know—a fantasy.*
—LINDA WELSCH

gain, from these beady-eyed parasites.) But it is not the worst
of the problems.

I have frequently taken the ridiculously perilous path of
buying tractors or machinery by mail or over the telephone,
and I suppose the results have been about the same—mostly nice
people selling honestly. When it is otherwise, of course, I have
no one to blame but myself. Nonetheless, I've grown a lot more
cautious about such deals, and I hope you'll be cautious too.

The worst example I've fallen into was the purchase of an
Allis G. Long before I knew or cared anything about old

tractors, I was introduced to the Model G Allis-Chalmers and could see at once what a nifty little machine it is. In fact, if I had a lot of money and wanted to make a hell of a lot more money, I would buy a factory and retool it to produce exact copies of the Allis G. Given the choice between that spiffy little garden-acreage-orchard tractor and the Russian and Japanese junk currently available on the market, only complete idiots would pass up the Welsch Model G.

Anyway, I got a letter from a guy who had read something I'd written, or saw something I did for television, and noted correctly that I am an Allis enthusiast. (Actually, I'm not an Allis enthusiast. I don't believe for a moment that the old Allis is better than any other old anything. It's the "old" I'm interested in and "tractor." The make isn't of any particular meaning to me.) He wrote that he had a G for sale. Wow! He sure got my attention. Along with a full set of six or eight implements! Yikes—just what I'd been looking for, and here it falls right into my lap. This guy's price was a little high, but with all those implements how could I go wrong?

Well the tractor didn't exactly fall into my lap. In fact it was actually 800 miles away, across two states. That pretty much ruled out the sale because I didn't even own a trailer, yet a vehicle suitable for hauling. But in an e-mail conversation with one of several tractor buddies, I mentioned the problem, and as I have found so often to be the case, one of them, Verne Holoubek, said, well, jeez, he'd go on the road to haul the tractor with me.

That makes the situation sound a lot simpler than it really was. Verne lives near Milwaukee. I live in the middle of Nebraska. The tractor was in Tennessee! I suppose I should be grateful that the tractor wasn't in Maine, that I don't live in Texas, and Verne doesn't live outside Seattle, but this

Milwaukee-Grand Island-Memphis triangle obviously wasn't going to work. No one drives that far to pick up a tractor.

Verne didn't seem to realize that, however. He blithely proceeded with arrangements despite my sputtering protestations. His plan was that I would drive to Lincoln, catch a plane to Chicago, where he would meet me with the truck and trailer, whereupon we would drive to Tennessee, pick up the tractor, haul it to Dannebrog, and then he would drive back to Milwaukee.

Now, we are talking here about thousands of miles. We are talking about airfare, gas, motels, food, and days of time. We are talking about driving through cities like St. Louis and Kansas City hauling a huge trailer with a tractor on it. Well this book is supposed to be about love, romance, relationships, sex, marriage, and, oh yeah, tractors. And this is definitely where love, romance, relationships, sex, and marriage come into play, believe me.

It is not easy to explain a project like this to a wife, whom you have just told that you really can't afford the time and expense of driving the 30 miles to Grand Island to see the movie *Something to Talk About,* the ultimate chick-flick and take her out to supper at that fancy new salad boutique, Fond o' Fondue, they've just built on the main drag. Right away, first thing, she's going to start drawing comparisons. There obviously is no comparison, you will argue. You are talking investment here, and uh, preserving a rare piece of agricultural history. And, er, accumulating material for another book . . . yeah, that's it—research for another book.

No matter what this trip is going to cost you, on top of the fairly hefty cost of the tractor—which, remember, you have yet to see—there will be no expense greater than what this all-too-necessary domestic negotiation will cost. Sure, you could take the easy way out and just shoot her, spend a couple of years in the slammer, and then come back to work on your G in your declining years, but ah, jeez, you're fond of her, and she sure can cook, and there is that other stuff you're just not going to get from a tractor, no matter how fond you are of it or how much care and devotion you lavish on it.

So you are pretty much reduced to other means. That is, crawling on your belly, whining and puling, begging, paying her off, making promises it will take you most of the rest of your life to pay off. And—agony of agonies—going to maybe 50 other films just as bad as and exactly as boring as *Something to Talk About* (no car chases, no explosions, lots of fade-outs, crashing waves, and sunsets just when things get interesting, if you know what I mean . . . and tell me, what kind of idiot can put together a film with Julia Roberts and not have her naked in a single scene?!) and eating and paying for God-knows-how-many terrible meals mostly made up of stuff you can't eat with your fingers and has never seen fire.

Okay, I laid that sort of foundation at home and got a note for Precious Moments from Verne's wife, Terri, that he would leadeth me not into temptation. And I did the same for him. (We did step a little out of bounds on two occasions, drifting astray into tractor "boneyards" in Illinois, where we lusted after parts and even touched some, but brought none home and made no commitments.) And we set off on Verne and Rog's Great Adventure.

I have a lot more to say about road trips later, so I will jump immediately to the kill on this one. With considerable ingenuity and effort we found the owner of the tractor and the machine itself. Hmmm. Well, it had clearly been compromised in some pretty dreadful ways. The gear shift cut off short, for example, and a canopy was welded on the top. It was running pretty rough, but well, here we were, 1,000 miles from home, and I had the money in my pocket, and it was, despite everything, an Allis G. We did have the truck and the trailer, and we'd really have some explaining to do when we got home if we went through all this only to come home empty-handed, so we set up to pay for and load the tractor.

Now, are we going to have room for all those implements? Blade, plow, lister, cultivator, disk harrow, tooth harrow, you know, all the stuff the guy told me about in his letter? The stuff that made the price acceptable? Maybe it's over there, behind that pile of twisted, rusty, junk rebar.

Yep, you guessed it. That pile of twisted, rusty, junk rebar was the implements. It was not what I had assumed, which was tractor implements. It was stuff slapped together that sort of served the purpose if you squinted your eyes and didn't turn on the lights too bright. We didn't even bother to load up most of it since the gas it would have taken to haul the stuff wouldn't have been worth the value of it as scrap iron.

Okay, it was my own fault. I could have asked, but I ignorantly presumed that when the tractor was advertised as coming with plow, harrow, cultivator, and so on, well, I kinda thought we were talking about a real plow, harrow, cultivator, and so on. My mistake.

But I'm still not at the real problem with this purchase, believe it or not. At this point I figured I was still doing all right. I did have a G (although at a pretty high price), and I had a couple of great days with a good buddy, and I had some super stories to add to my collection of tractor anecdotes. No, the real problems with this situation were yet to come and were going to last a while.

It's one thing when a person selling a tractor has an attachment to the machine and wants to keep track of it. I can understand that. But some folks figure that they are one of the implements you'll take along with you when you load up that tractor and drive off with it. Okay, you've been warned. Make sure if you are buying a tractor or implements that you have a clear idea what you are getting. And when you buy a tractor, make sure that's all you're getting and not somehow buying the owner right along with the machine.

MATCHES MADE IN HEAVEN

Nor should you for a moment think that my horror story is typical. If anything, I am surprised how often people I get tractors from really do turn out to be good, honest sellers who eventually do become friends of mine. I have a lot of downright heart-warming stories along that line, but maybe my favorite is about the very first Allis WC I ever owned. I've told the story often enough in enough places that I won't bother you with the whole thing again, but a friend gave me Sweet Allis and I came to love her. I learned from the donor that the tractor had originally belonged to Don and Bernice Jeffries, who are parents of another friend of mine, Jan Jeffries. Well that was something of a surprise, and a pleasant one: It's nice to know something of the heritage of a love interest like Sweet Allis.

I heard along the line somewhere, probably from Jan, that her folks were leaving the farm and I may have even said something about being interested in any implements or parts they might have, since they were pretty much Allis-Chalmers farmers. But I certainly didn't pursue the issue or really think much about it. Eventually I got a note from Don that he did indeed have some Allis parts, a carburetor or two, a magneto, some pistons, a block, other bits and pieces. Would I be interested in them?

Sure. I'm always interested in parts. Parts are expensive; new parts are utterly out of reach in many cases. I was a trifle uneasy that we made arrangements for Don to haul a trailer of parts out here without having discussed prices, but you know, it would be nice to have parts from Sweet Allis' original daddy, and well, these are nice people, and gosh, well, you know how those things go. We just didn't get around to discussing prices.

When they drove in the yard, I could see they were hauling treasures. There were lots of good parts on that trailer, even a couple of brand-new parts. I recall, for example, a camshaft still in its original waxed paper wrapping. Still without really doing much by way of setting prices or conditions, we started unloading the parts into my shop. I almost dreaded to hear what Don thought this was all worth. Frankly, I couldn't afford to pay what it was all worth.

> Women are like elephants to me.
> I like to look at them, but I wouldn't
> want to own one.
> —W. C. FIELDS

Finally the clumsy moment came when we were pretty much reduced to saying good-byes and, uh, writing a check. We stood there, twisting our big toes in the dust a while, and finally Don said something like, "Well, would you be willing to pay $100 for the load?"

I may be wrong on that price. It may have been something exorbitant like $150. I do remember that his asking price really wouldn't cover the mileage of bringing the stuff into our yard.

You know, I realized pretty much on the spot what was really happening. He wasn't selling me those parts. He was giving them to me. But he was sparing us both the trouble of dealing with a gift of that magnitude. You know, all those protestations, and thank yous, and gratitude, and all those clumsy sorts of things that go along with an extravagant gift. This way the deal was strictly business. Yeah, right.

As they drove out of our yard with the empty wagon, Don slowed down and opened his window. I approached the pick-up. "You wouldn't be interested in a WD, would you?"

Hmmm. I didn't have an Allis-Chalmers Model WD tractor. Sure would like to have a WD, though, especially from the very man who had farmed for so long with my favorite tractor, Sweet Allis. And I had a very good idea of how Don cared for his tractors (like loved children) so this tractor was probably in prime condition. But I never really intended to accumulate models across the Allis line; I was interested only in WC Model Allises. And I didn't . . . don't . . . have a lot of money to throw around. Just as was the case with the parts, I would've liked to have a WD but quite honestly couldn't pay what a WD is worth.

"Uh, well, sure, I guess so. What are you going to need for it?"

"How would you feel about $600?"

So, here we are, another case of buying a tractor sight unseen. While $600 would have been a good price for any Allis WD, and I had reason to suspect that this tractor might be a good buy, I really didn't need a WD, and I really didn't have $600 to spare, and I did need to think about using the money more wisely on tools I needed and buying parts for fixing up WCs I was already committed to work on. The purchase of this WD would make no sense at all. So of course I said, "Sure. I'll take it."

Don and Bernice hauled her (note the gender reference once she's mine!) out to our place a few weeks later, and she was a wonderful buy. As a matter of fact, she wound up being the model for a high-class painting and print by the world-famous wildlife and tractor artist Neil Anderson! Now she rests comfortably nestled alongside her sister, Sweet Allis. This was obviously a good deal, for both me and Don Jeffries. He found a good home for his WD. I got a lovely tractor, and we came away from our curious bargaining both very happy and both, in fact, good friends.

PRACTICAL PROCUREMENTS

Other times, some such transactions come down to nothing more than money. That's okay too. I've bought tractors from scrap yards, at auctions, and from individuals strictly on a cash-on-the-barrel head basis. Nothing wrong with that. The seller wants the most he can get out of his iron; the buyer wants as good a buy as he can get. The seller has some notion of his bottom line; the buyer should have a clear idea of his top price. If you can't come together, no hard feelings. If you make a bargain, okay, you both retreat to assess how you've done, and hopefully you both come away feeling you did okay. If you didn't, you have no one to blame but yourself.

Sometimes I have gotten bargains like this, sometimes I haven't. The problem arises when the seller thinks he has a real treasure to sell, or a real sucker as a customer.

Sellers should be aware, or be made aware, that the fact that this machine meant something to the family means damn little to most buyers. I can't buy someone else's sentiment. If either the seller or the buyer is ignorant—thinking he has a real prize worth a fortune when really it's fairly common junk, or that he's going to steal something of value from someone too dumb to know the difference—the best thing is to beat a hasty retreat as quickly as possible. No one is going to come out happy from a process like that. There are going to be hard feelings, maybe even when the transaction isn't closed, and that simply isn't worth the time, trouble, or vexation. You'll never be happy working or riding on a tractor that came out of an angry bargain.

Same for the other side of that coin: I really am uncomfortable with the idea of bilking some poor widder lady out'n the mint-condition Ford 8-N her late and lamented husband bought and drove into the barn. But then he stumbled over a milk bucket and fell into the horse stall, where a skittish mare stomped him into the manure like a grape in an Eye-talian wine vat. Moreover, I don't think that happens all that often. In fact, now that I think about it, I don't believe I have ever encountered a situation where I had to feel guilty about bilking any guileless innocent out of anything. Except Lovely Linda, and I'm not so sure she was all that innocent. In fact, now that I really think about it . . .

About the only time I can recall feeling a twinge of guilt in buying a tractor was when I bought a pretty little Farmall Cub from a woman who had just split up with her husband. It was his tractor, and she was selling it. I did hesitate for a moment, wracked by my overzealous conscience. Then I gave the issue some serious thought and came up with something like, "Well, she's going to sell this thing to someone, and it might just be someone who isn't really a very nice guy and won't appreciate what a nice little tractor this is. On the other hand, there's me, and I'm a real sweetheart, and I am precisely the kind of guy I would want to have my tractors, so I'm sure (pretty sure, anyway) this guy would want someone like me to get his tractor. And maybe if I pay for it in cash and give her a phony name, he'll never know where it went anyway."

But it's not like I didn't think about the morality of the issue at all, and it's the thought that counts. I think that's in the Bible somewhere.

I'm still at a total loss to figure out people who buy tractors already restored to immaculate condition, probably well beyond the purity of the blasted machines when they rolled off the assembly line. (They are meant to haul manure spreaders and drag plows, after all.) I guess they like to look at them, and I know some folks get a kick out of driving them in parades and such. But I don't see what kind of pleasure people get out of driving a tractor they own but have had nothing to do with any more than I understand someone taking pride in a new car. You didn't do anything but pay for the damned thing, after all. If that proves anything, it only shows that you're an idiot who has no comprehension whatsoever of the concept of depreciation. "There goes a guy in a new car. He must have more money than brains." That's all that goes through my mind.

A REAL LIFE FAIRY TALE

Now that I've said that, I can offer up what I consider to be a solid exception, who just happens to be my father-in-law, Jake. It's not just that I want to stay on his good side and well situated in the will: Jake's a Catholic, after all. By the time we get done splitting up his estate, there won't be enough for each of us to buy our way into a movie. A matinee, maybe, and I got his pretty daughter already, so that isn't really the issue.

While I once lusted after his beautiful John Deere B, one of his sons, Steve, has ever-so-subtly named his children Jacob, Jacobette, Jacobina, Jakelet, Jakeline, Jake, and Jakelee. I think Steve pretty much has a corner on that tractor, therefore—and the house and car. And the $23 U.S. savings bond Jake keeps under his mattress.

It's a real romantical story. Jake was driving from his folks' farm near Dwight, Nebraska, to his first day at his new job at the Goodyear Rubber Company factory in Lincoln. Along the way he passed a farm implement dealer's lot and saw this John Deere B sitting on the lot. It wasn't new but darn near. He stopped by with his first paycheck and bought that tractor. (Remember: This was a long time ago. Jake has since retired from Goodyear!) It served his father as a good workhorse, and then Jake, and Jake kept track of that machine. After all, it was his.

Then he retired from Goodyear and the kids moved out and he and Sally got a nice suburban home on the outskirts of Lincoln and, well, he's never said as much, but I think he decided then it was payback time. He isn't really a mechanic himself, and he's not into restoration. But he wanted to do something for himself and his family, and doggone it, let's face it, that good ol' tractor. So he bought the Old Girl a full makeover, just like they do on *Oprah*.

Now, there are going to be some of you, since you are men, who don't watch *Oprah*, especially when she has makeovers. As a part of the sacrifices I've made to produce this book for you, I agonized through a week's worth of *Oprah* shows, including the makeovers. A makeover is when a real ugly woman is selected from the audience (or sometimes offered up by her family) to be spiffed up by professionals with names like "Mr. Enree" or "Bruce," but spelled funny, like "Brooss" or "Bruis" or "Bruz."

These guys do to the road-weary lady pretty much what you and I do with a battered old tractor: They do a little work on the sheet metal, spray some refresher on the tires, replace the belts and hoses, hose her down with a stream-pressure washer, and repaint her. You know, what the fancy guys at the used car lot call "detailing." Then they parade the lady out on the stage, show a "before" picture, and then everyone goes crazy about how fancy she is now with a little attention and care.

That's what Jake did with his John Deere B. And just like those much abused, tired ladies on Oprah, that John Deere deserved that kind of treatment. When she was all fixed up, man, she was pretty. Jake has a brand spanking new, red Pontiac Grand Prix sitting in his garage. Now, right next to it, proud as can be, that John Deere B he bought 50 years ago.

Didn't I tell you the story was plum romantical? Almost makes me want to cry. Especially the part about Steve naming all those kids.

CHAPTER 6

THE MAGICAL
MYSTICAL
TRACTOR
ROAD TRIP

*The reason husbands and wives do not understand each other
is because they belong to different sexes.*
—DOROTHY DIX

Richard Fool Bull was a wonderful old gentleman, an elder and wise man of the Lakota Tribe. This guy was truly magic. He knew so many things that the rest of us simply cannot imagine, but what's more, he had a terrific sense of humor. I can't remember how the topic came up, but we once drifted somehow into the area of love, marriage, romance, and sex (but, in this case, not tractors) and he set me straight on polygamy.

He told me that white guys are always drooling about the idea that a Lakota warrior might have two, three, even four wives. He said it was a matter of good economics; it might take that many women to keep an active hunter-warrior in clothing, shelter, and food. In the winter it contributed to comfort to roll up in a buffalo robe with three or four women at once.

Mr. Fool Bull paused to let that image soak in, and to let me drool a little maybe, and then he added, a form of punctuation right up there with the atomic bomb, "All sisters."

"Three or four sisters," he said again.

My God. That means that when you left the toilet seat up, or tracked mud into the kitchen, or didn't sort the laundry exactly right (men, I will try to explain this sorting laundry thing a little better in the chapter devoted to women, hidden toward the back of this book, but believe me, when women talk about sorting laundry, they aren't thinking of tractor parts in one pile, overalls in another). Where was I? Oh yeah. That means that when you screwed up in a Lakota tipi, you didn't have just one woman mad at you, you had a tag-team of four, all thinking exactly alike, all raised the same way, now brace yourself . . . ALL WITH THE SAME MOTHER!!!

While I'm at it, let me burst yet another bubble from your group-grope fantasies. Brigham Young had something like 25 wives. (I'd check on that, but maybe even he wasn't sure how many there were. I mean, how do you keep track? Ear tags?) I have an acquaintance, a historical researcher whose name will remain unrevealed here since he is a Mormon, and the story I'm about to tell you may not be precisely the sort of thing the Church will want to have out and about. (Makes a religious icon look much too human, don't you know?)

Anyway, this scholar-friend of mine was doing some research on the records of a very early cabinetmaker in the new Mormon colony of Salt Lake City in its earliest years. This woodworker kept detailed records of everything he did, all the expenses and sales, all the requests and requirements. My friend said that he was particularly excited when he came across an entry in the records where the cabinetmaker had a visit from The Man Himself, Brigham Young, requesting that a special cedar and oak vanity chest be made as a present for a particularly favored new bride of his. This item was really fancy, with lovely, delicate decorations, shiny brass hinges and hasp. You know, the very kind of thing *you* would give to a special new woman in your life.

And the craftsman recorded that Brigham Young came by to pick up the finished *objet d'art*, was mighty pleased, paid for it, and carried it off, almost certainly with an eye toward pleasing this new bedmate in his life.

Pretty neat, huh? Isn't that what you would do if you were lucky enough to have 25 wives and had just picked up a new little lovely to add to your collection? Well, get this: As my friend continued on his way through the cabinetmaker's accounting book, he found just a couple of pages later where Brigham Young returned to the shop, with a new order. For 25 more fancy cedar boxes. Just like the first.

Now, I want you to think on that. Develop the scene in your mind. Can you imagine what hit the fan when ol' Brig came home with that first fancy trinket for the new cutie in the household? Can you conjure up an image of the hell he went through before he groaned and hauled himself back into the wagon to go back to that woodworker to order up 25 more? It must be a lot of fun to have a bunch of wives. Oh, yeah, and sticking a hornet's nest down the front of your overalls will sure focus your attention on the important things in life.

Having apparently learned nothing, Brigham Young eventually wound up with, brace yourself, 56 wives. Right offhand, I'd guess that's why the Mormons called themselves "saints."

Anyway, Mr. Fool Bull ended his enlightening story by noting that another thing white guys always seem to wonder about the finest horsemen the Plains ever saw, is why they

were always running off to hunt buffalo or kick some innocent Pawnee's shins. Four sisters at home, in the same tipi.
With the same mother. That's why.

Essentially, what you did, Running Scared, is come back
only when you needed (1) a warm meal, (2) clean socks, and
(3) a good, solid reminder of why you ran off with the boys
to hunt buffalo three moons ago. And man, then you didn't
waste any time at all in figuring out some good reason to ride
over the horizon again with a bunch of buddies. I'll bet you
rode that first day until you could no longer hear the sounds
of squalling babies, arguing sisters, and a mother-in-law
reminding her girls once again what she'd said about you the
first time you tied your pony outside the family digs.

This is not a one-way road. I am told, sometimes color-
fully, that there are times in a woman's life, most of the time
in a woman's life, when she would just as soon not share male
company. Hard to imagine, but take it from me; I'm the guy
writing the book.

The frankest I have ever heard expressed about this side
of the issue was by a little old lady I met a few years ago. She
almost assuredly violated the Basic Rules of Woman School by
telling me this, but I think she figured she was old enough
that she no longer needed to worry about the Death to Big-
Mouth Sisters Rule.

Anyway, this woman and her husband, still married after
60 years of wedded blitz [sic], told me the touching story of
how they both migrated to this country from Denmark and
worked as hired hands on a Wisconsin farm, where they met
and courted. Sven finally popped the question to her, she
said as she smiled coyly, and he added, "Lena, I'd like to ask
ya to be my vedded vife. I'll do my best to be a good man to
ya, even dow I know I'm not a very handsome gent."

She told me that she replied without hesitation, "Sure, I'll marry you, Sven. You'll be out in the fields most of the time anyway."

Which brings us to why tractor guys take road trips to haul tractors. Thing is, all women are sisters. They go to Woman School, and they all stick together. Men stumble through their lives, each inventing all over again the idea of getting the hell out of the house. NASCAR, pheasant hunting, fishing, jobs, tractors, whatever it is that can get them to the relative peace and quiet of screaming engines, shotgun blasts, factory pollution, and filthy oil. They never seem to arrive at the obvious and valuable fact that such protracted absences from the domestic scene are good for a relationship. (Unfortunately, the relationship in question is often between the wife and the UPS delivery guy, but that's another issue.)

I may be wrong. The venerated Tractor Road Trip may actually fall more into the category of the Native American vision quest. Fetching and hauling a tractor is more mystic and holy than warfare and hunting. Especially the first 10 minutes. I have gone on maybe 15 Tractor Hauling Trips, hereafter to be identified as THTs. THTs are fun from the very first moment you smash a fingernail hitching the trailer until the very last moment when you proudly unload your prize in the backyard and find that the carb, mag, distributor cap, and anything else virtually irreplaceable vibrated loose and fell off somewhere along the journey.

But nothing, NOTHING is like the very first moment of total freedom you feel when your buddy pushes his pickup into drive. You look at each other, grin a stupid grin, and set off for a couple of days of utterly wasted time, mechanical disaster, financial idiocy, and scenery that features mostly rust, rotten rubber, and the possible remnants of a tractor buried under six generations of dirt and grease. Every moment of a THT is good; that moment is best.

If you have never been on a THT, I'm going to tell you about some right now. And then, if you've never been on a THT, you are going to be looking around for some reason to go on one, I promise you. Am I exaggerating? Ask someone who's been on a THT, or consider if you yourself have been on one, the looks in the eyes of men in other vehicles as they passed you or you passed by them. Haunting, isn't it? It's the look a black lab has in his eyes when he sees a pickup truck loaded with guys dressed in camouflage gear, shotguns, and other dogs headed toward the country. They're going hunting and he's not. You're on a THT and the other guy isn't. It's heartbreaking, sure, but you just have to tell yourself that this is your THT, and sooner or later there will be a THT for the other black lab, uh, tractor guy.

CAUTION: It doesn't work to go on a THT on your own. Sure, it's sort of fun, but not enough fun. You can tell She Who Must Be Obeyed that the reason there has to be a pickup load of guys to pick up one tractor is safety. She'll accept that, even though she may have some further questions about the cooler of cold beer in the back of the truck.

The reason safety is not all that crucial is that you are going to have disaster no matter what. The real reason for multi-staffing THTs is witnesses. I once hauled an Allis WC home from an auction sale just 30 miles up the road in Loup City. It was so close, I didn't really need any help.

Dumb. I needed a witness. I could tell the story myself of what it took to get that damn piece-of-junk tractor pulled up into the damn piece-of-junk front-wheel dolly I bought at another auction sale, and I could tell the story about how whenever I approached 20 miles per hour the back end of that

Allis proceeded to bounce 10 feet into the air, almost tearing my pickup truck in half. And I could tell about how I therefore had to go onto gravel roads for a good 20 miles to avoid meeting a state trooper or anyone else with sense who would force me off the road. Or I could tell about how then the tractor bounced back and forth instead of up and down and cleared every grain of gravel off that road from Ashton to Dannebrog. But somehow, it just isn't the same without a witness.

There's not a doubt in my mind that it was the same with the Indians. It wasn't just nailing a buffalo or bringing home a Ponca scalp. No, I firmly believe that the fun was coming home with your buddies and sitting around the fire, laughing about how funny it was when you shot a buffalo just as he was making successful advances on another bull's cow, or bonking that Ponca just as he thought he'd found a nice private place for an evening contemplative, if you catch my drift. Or, more likely, about how Pawnee Killer shot himself in the foot with an arrow, or Dances With Guys fell in the creek while sneaking up on the Cheyenne village and couldn't get his breechcloth off before it shrank up and had him making war cries in a soprano voice.

Witnesses.

TWICE THE ADVENTURE

A locally famous THT I took with a couple of buddies whose names will not be revealed here for perfectly obvious reasons (let's call them Woodrow and Bunkie) had, for example, two beginnings. Three weeks apart. The first time we took off on a clear, pretty, autumn day for a little town in Kansas where I had purchased, sight unseen, two Allis WCs from a junkyard. It was a long trip, maybe 15 hours total, so we started early. We enjoyed the Golden Moment of

Departure (hereafter to be indicated as GMD) and gleefully set off to find adventure.

It didn't take long. We were dragging Bunkie's trailer, always a source of anecdotal excitement. The tires were (still are) bald and several need to be aired up every hour or so; parts tend to fall off so we had to stop every hour whether the tires need airing or not to resecure things like chains, chocks, ramps, and the tongue. We were spared the problem of worrying how to manage this moving wreck on highways by virtue of the fact that Bunkie fills his pickup, which is in pretty much the same condition as his trailer, with illegal diesel fuel meant for agricultural work, not highway travel.

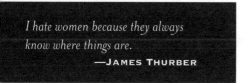

I hate women because they always know where things are.
—JAMES THURBER

For those of you not familiar with agricultural systems, these two fuels come in different colors (no kidding) so authorities can check and see if you are burning the low-taxed fuel or the more heavily burdened highway stuff. And they aren't at all understanding when they catch you fudging.

Bunkie fudges, which means we have to avoid troopers. By traveling on gravel roads. Hundreds of miles, picking our way county by county along unknown paths and underengineered bridges. It is a scenario designed for adventure, believe me.

Well, on this occasion we hadn't gone 10 miles before our adventures began. Every time Bunkie hit the brakes to go into a curve in the road, everything went crazy. There was a ferocious, slamming vibration that shook us to our tonsils. We tried to guess. Brake linings falling apart? Master cylinder shelling out? Transmission maybe? We got out, like real men do, and looked. We crawled under everything. We kicked things. Nothing seemed responsible for the hiccups.

We started off again. Same problem. Forty miles out we were so rattled, our eyes had crossed, the beer cans had blown up in the cooler, and it was clear there was no way we could haul a tractor 250 miles like this, let alone to Kansas to pick them up in the first place. After 50 miles we gave up and pulled over. We had, in fact, even gone too far to make it back to my house in this condition.

So we called up Kenny Porath, a master mechanic and the only person other than myself so innocent of wrongdoing that I can use his real name in this narrative. He came out, did some repairs on the engine (which had been shaken pretty much out of whack by that time), and tried to assess our problems so we could limp back to Dannebrog. (Even if we got this parade back on the road now it was too late to make the trip to Kansas. We had no option but the humiliation of returning disgraced to our tipis. Uh, farms.)

Kenny got the engine back into running condition and then considered our transmission/brake/whatever problem. Actually, he found it rather quickly. Seems Bunkie had hooked up the trailer's electric brakes to the pickup's electrical system in such a way that they operated not when the brake lights came on but when the turn signals came on. And off and on and off and on and off and on and off. WHAM WHAM WHAM WHAM WHAM WHAM WHAM.

Now, the thing is, we did not come home empty-handed. We had a really great story. Better yet, Woodrow and I were innocent bystanders and the idiot, in this particular case, was Bunkie. That's a good kind of story, if you're not Bunkie.

We eventually started this trip all over again a few weeks later, the engine duct-taped back together and the trailer brakes coordinated this time to the truck brakes. Another

THT, another GMD, another pretty dawning, another splendid adventure. We stopped at a McDonald's and service station
50 miles into the trip to get some breakfast, air the trailer tires,
and get some information about gravel headed south into
Kansas. So far, so good, but adventure was sneaking up on us,
even without our knowing.

I had an egg-sausage McMuffin and hashbrowns. I love
McDonald's egg-sausage McMuffins and hashbrowns.
Woodrow had the same. We all got a big cup of hot coffee.
Bunkie ate his customary day-starter—eight breakfast burritos.
Bunkie is a big boy, and I think you can now probably see
where I am going with this, right?

Well, we got to this tiny town in north-central Kansas,
found my buddy who'd lined up this splendid deal for me
(he's a dentist, always a good source of tractor information),
and went out to the junkyard to take a look. It was enough to
make a grown man cry. Two total wrecks, not a decent part on
either one, let alone a restorable tractor, and I paid for each
what I wouldn't have paid for both. Tuition. That's what I call
it when I wind up making a mistake this stupid: tuition. You
pay your fees and you get your education.

We winched this dead iron up onto Bunkie's trailer,
chained them down (as if they would roll anywhere!), and
refilled the tires for the 32nd time that day. We were about to
crawl back into the pickup when the junkyard guy, who hadn't
lifted a finger to help us through this entire operation, said,
"Then you don't want the wheels?"

Hmmm. There were remnants of wheels on the tractors
we had just loaded, but I've paid a lot of tuition over the
years, so I've had a lot of lessons. "Uh, well, let's take a look
and see if we have room for them," I tiptoed. He walked us
through the rubble and ruin of his yard, way to the back, up

a hill. I could tell that no matter what he had, we sure as hell weren't going to be able to get up this hill with the trailer and truck and through the junk to get whatever wheels he had in mind, not to mention that in our entire walk I didn't spot a single useable item in his whole inventory. Nothing but scrap iron, if that.

And then I saw them.

It was like that TV ad where the old guy and the beautiful woman run toward each other in slow motion and into each other's arms. I think it's a Viagra ad. No, wait a minute, Viagra makes you dance, not run. (Lovely Linda says she's holding out for a pill that makes men not just dance, but line dance. They're never gonna make that pill for me. My theory is that this younger age is willing to do close order drill to a whiny southern voice only because they never spent time in the military. One good war and that country and western line dancing nonsense is as good as dead.)

To get back to my story, I saw them: four iron wheels. Not just wheels like the ones you mount rubber on. No, these are iron wheels. With lugs. And not just iron lug wheels either. These were sublime, iron, lugged wheels. One was a set of "spider wheels," very rare for this area. I've never seen one for sale, as a matter of fact. And the others were a kind of double-spider wheel I'd never seen before and haven't seen since. These things are so gorgeous I have seriously thought about making front room lamps out of them. (But not so gorgeous that I've suggested to Lovely Linda we put those lamps in our front room.)

"Uh, yeah," I said as casually as I could, and hoping this backwoods yahoo couldn't hear the sweat popping out of my forehead, I yawned. "Uuuuh, I suppose we could find room for those on the trailer. Maybe just for ballast, if nothing else." I picked up two of the wheels, tucked them under my arms, and ran back to the trailer, trying not to look too eager, and then ran back and met Woodrow and Bunkie rolling the other wheels back to the truck. They had clearly been impressed to see an old, fat guy pick up a half ton of iron like that and run with it.

"Not so damn slow," I hissed. "We gotta get these things loaded before someone tells him we're stealing them." And I picked up the other two and ran back to the trailer with them. Okay, maybe I'm exaggerating just a little here, but not much.

"Start the truck," I snarled at Bunkie. "Right now, you idiot. Start the truck and get out of here." Somewhat startled by this attitude from Mr. Easy, he started up and pulled out of the junkyard.

Since it had taken us almost a half hour to get to the wheels and get them back to the trailer, the tires of Bunkie's trailer needed airing up again and we needed fuel too, so we pulled into a co-op station on the outskirts of town. Woodrow and I did what we could to get air into the tires faster than it could leak out while Bunkie went to the office to pay for the fuel, buy a candy bar, and do whatever else he needed to do before we set off, heading up 250 miles of gravel road toward home. (Even with the admixture of new fuel, our tanks wouldn't have passed inspection, so we all knew it would be a long, dusty, bumpy ride on gravel roads back to my place, now with a load of junk tractors and treasure-wheels.)

Then it was Bunkie's turn. About 10 minutes later he came running from the direction of the office, and I want to tell you, seeing Bunkie run is for all the world like watching a gigantic avalanche. I imagine he weighs in at about 320, but we can't be sure since the truck scale up at the elevator went bad. Anyway, here he came on the dead run, and he had a look of urgency now on his face.

"Get in the truck," he hissed. "We gotta go now, and I mean right now."

Woodrow was still kneeling alongside a soggy tire and said, "Just a minute. I'll have this tire aired up in a sec."

"Forget the damn tire. Get in the truck NOW, or I'm leaving without you."

Well, there was obviously some need for haste here, so Woodrow and I threw ourselves into the cab of Bunkie's truck, and just in time, because he had, in one motion, started the truck, thrown it into gear, and slammed the accelerator to the floor. He didn't even look for a gravel road. He just headed down that highway, illegal fuel and all, doing everything he could to get that truck, trailer, and tractors as far above the speed limit as he could go.

I suppose we were 15 miles down the road before that engine dropped back to an rpm level we could talk over, but even then Woodrow and I didn't ask what was going on. We could deal with crises. You know, warm beer, no fishing license, gas in a closed tent, things like that. But we could tell this was something we had to leave up to Bunkie to deal with. He would have to decide when and what to tell us, but we couldn't help but wonder.

Later we compared notes about our thoughts at that moment: Had Bunkie held up the service station, and if so, why didn't he grab two more candy bars? Were we going to be charged with stealing compressed air? Had someone finally figured out that we were stealing those iron wheels?

Eventually, maybe a half hour out, we slowed down to a safe pace on the gravel and Bunkie, biting his lip, decided to unload his conscience. It was the breakfast burritos. After saying hello to the guys loafing in the station, and buying his candy bar, he went into the men's room. And unloaded breakfast. Not to mention the lunch of braunschweiger sandwiches, crispy Cheetos, and apple pie Lovely Linda had sent along. And a bunch of jerky from the last deer season that Bunkie happened to still have in his glovebox.

I just don't know how to discuss this event delicately, but if the sissy who edits and publishes this book follows my advice, this book won't be made available for sale to women anyway, so I guess I'm safe. Thing is, Bunkie had rid himself of the entire day's gut bombs in one fell swoop, in that pitiful little service station's domestic-grade toilet, which is for all the world like fueling an Allis-Chalmers WC field tractor with nitro-methane.

It was total destruction. At least that's what Bunkie told us. He had no reason to lie, and we had no reason to doubt his account. Now we understood his anxiety. For all we knew, that service station had the Kansas State Patrol out looking for us at this very moment. Maybe even an EPA SWAT team. The least of our problems was illegal fuel. I don't even know what the penalty would be for destroying a small-town service station privy.

Well, once we crossed the state line, we slowed down and turned onto the gravel. Never did do anything with the tractors. They're still sitting here, right outside my window. Or the wheels, although I admire them regularly. We sure have gotten a lot of mileage out of the story about Bunkie and those breakfast burritos.

GUINNESS RECORDS ROAD TRIPS

The shortest THT I've ever made was with Mel Halsey, all the way to Grand Island 30 miles south. On that occasion we had to hand-winch a wreck out of a bog, back behind a bunch of trees, but we got it done and got the tractor home. We had our GMD, talked a lot of philosophy, had a few beers, only hurt ourselves a little, and generally convinced Sue and Linda that we really had been working hard all day. You gotta count that as a good day.

I already told you a little about the longest trip, the Dannebrog-Lincoln-Chicago-Tennessee-St. Louis-Kansas City-Dannebrog (and then back to Milwaukee for Verne!) THT that Verne Holoubek and I made to pick up the Allis G. If you haven't done a trip like that, you just cannot imagine how pleasant it is to be driving along with a good buddy, talking, eating junk food, enjoying some beautiful scenery, anticipating picking up an interesting tractor, and then on the way home laughing at what idiots you are. In fact, the whole process was so funny, after five days of driving, eating, and talking, all Verne and I had to do was sit there and listen to the radio, watch the scenery, and every so often look over at each other, knowing precisely what the other was thinking, and start laughing so hard root beer came out our respective noses.

There was also a certain charm in driving through St. Louis and Kansas City precisely in the evening rush hours of both cities, with that huge trailer under a thoroughly goofy tractor. The looks from the yuppies were at best amusement, at worst contempt. But there were others: men who knew not only what we had in that tractor, but also what fun we were having making that trip, who looked at us wistfully, sadly. We simply couldn't bring ourselves to do anything in those cases but shrug a shoulder and give a thumbs up. A kinda "Hang in there, pal. Someday you'll be in a pickup truck with a good buddy hauling a classic tractor through a big city rush hour and eating crap too." They won't, of course, but it didn't hurt to give them hope.

Probably the most uncomfortable moment of the trip was totally unexpected. We stopped at a tractor boneyard in a small Illinois town a little south of St. Louis and walked among the wreckage with the proprietor. It was a nice yard, and there were a lot of things there we would have liked to have hauled away if we'd had the money and the room. Verne did pick up a couple of minor parts for a combine, and we went to the office to pay for them.

That's when we made the mistake: Verne introduced me. Up to that moment I'd just been the half-wit brother sitting in the passenger seat, but they recognized the name. They knew that I was the guy who had just that month written a column in *Successful Farming* magazine about how to deal with salvage/junkyard/scrap yard owners. I thought I was being funny when I wrote it.

After all, I have a good friend who runs a salvage yard, and we pass the same jokes back and forth all the time. You know, I ask him about a 2-inch long 1/2-inch bolt, and he says, hmmm, those are getting really hard to find, and then he picks one off the ground and charges me $3 for it. When I go to him and take some parts off his "parters," he looks at what I've taken, tells me the bill is $60, and he'll just let me go ahead and take for nothing the stuff I stole and stuck under the front seat.

Well, the folks running this salvage yard didn't find jokes like that so funny. It was a trifle uncomfortable, but we got out with our skins. Then, all the way from Illinois to Nebraska, for two days, there was all the more reason for Verne and me to look over at each other every hour or so and start to giggle.

There are lots of ways to move a tractor, but the bed of a truck or trailer is definitely the best. A former friend of mine once rode a purchase of mine back from a sale, towed behind a truck. Twenty miles. Consider for a moment the suspension system of the Allis-Chalmers WC tractor. There isn't any, unless you count a few inches of rock-hard old rubber in the tire. Some WC seats are mounted on a big spring with what looks like a shock absorber up the inside. Not this one. The iron seat sits on the end of 18 inches of solid, unyielding steel. The only thing between this guy's bony butt and the road was the thickness of his overalls. He won't speak to me to this day, and who can blame him?

TRACTORS AND THE UNEXPLAINED

Another tractor I had rebuilt and pretty much finished up still wasn't running right and a local master mechanic, Melvin Nelson, kindly offered to take a look at it over at this shop. While he was it, he hauled it over there on his tilt-bed truck. That's the way to do it, but after he had tuned it up and got some magneto problems sorted out, Woodrow, Lunchbox, and I decided that he'd gone to far too much trouble already, so we'd just drive her the 6 miles back to my place. Woodrow assured us it would be an easy, even pleasant trip. It was only a matter of 5 or 6 miles, after all.

I guess I had forgotten about the time Woodrow offered to help me bring a disk harrow I'd been given back to my place. I couldn't imagine how we were going to load that brute, but he told me not to worry about it. He sure didn't. We just hooked that harrow up behind his Scout and drove the country road back to town, pretty much harrowing all 5 miles of county gravel. Until we got to town. Then we threw sparks from the highway pavement and started grassfires until we finally reached the safe haven—and anonymity—of my driveway. I'm not going to ask you to try to imagine the sound of a disk harrow going 40 miles an hour down a paved highway; I don't think you can do that without having witnessed such a thing.

Or the consequences to the harrow. As I recall, as we unhitched what was left, Woodrow wet a finger and touched the nearly red-hot disks and remarked, "That gravel pretty well cleans up a harrow, now, doesn't it?"

Back to getting the tractor from Melvin Nelson's place to mine. Woodrow's a good guy, and pretty smart, but he does things in ways you might not expect, since you, like me, probably feel constrained by the laws of physics, those of the state of Nebraska (or fill in your own state), and common sense.

While Lunchbox and I finished up details with Melvin, Woodrow decided he would start off down the gravel road toward my place on the newly rejuvenated tractor, which I had dubbed the Woodpecker. (It's the very same tractor I wrote about in *Busted Tractors and Rusty Knuckles*.) I reckon he made 500 yards on the first leg; he was still in sight when we saw the tractor slow to a stop and Woodrow heave himself off the iron seat. By the time we got to him, he had dismantled the fuel system with a pocketknife and was blowing great gobs of black goo out of the lines and carburetor.

MORAL: Never empty a can of gas into a vehicle's gas tank. Generations of goop, gunk, glop, and glick will have settled to the bottom of that can and while they may be by-products of gasoline, they do not flow or burn like gasoline.

It didn't take these tractor-lovin' farm boys long to get that tractor back together and running and we set off again, Woodrow driving, Lunchbox and me following in Lunchbox's pickup truck. From behind, we could see quite clearly that there were some wheel and tire problems I had apparently not addressed in the two-year process of rebuilding the Woodpecker.

We stopped now and then to pick up pieces shaken loose from the tractor while Woodrow plowed straight ahead. As long as that thing was running and rolling, he figured the best plan was to keep heading right down that gravel. The front tires left a skittish track in the dust and gravel that looked for all the world like that of a gigantic anaconda snake. The front of that tractor was making pretty much the same pattern in the air.

The back tires were moving along in two straight lines, but ever larger hunks of rubber were flying off, to the point where Lunchbox and I finally had to drop back another 30 yards and turn on the windshield wipers. Not to mention that every so often the Woodpecker backfired and belched a mighty cloud of white and black smoke. (I know that sounds unlikely, black and white smoke, but no kidding; that's exactly what she was belching.) Various fluids dripped, ran, spurted, and oozed from places on that tractor I didn't know even contained liquids. "The Welsch tractor's snaky path was flanked by two trails of black, rubber litter, nicely glazed with a drizzled frosting of fluids of richly varied viscosity," is how the social column read the next week in the Dannebrog newspaper.

Now, here's one of the many, many, many reasons a tractor is referred to with the feminine pronoun: While we were enormously gratified that she made 6 miles on that shaky front end (you'll have to read *Busted Tractors and Rusty Knuckles* to find out how I solved that problem), flaking rear tires, losing various effluviates, and with the engine burping, she chose precisely the most embarrassing place possible to finally cough her last cough. Or perhaps more precisely, laugh her last laugh.

Almost within sight of my shop, but more important, in full view of the entire village of Dannebrog on a state highway that was, at the time, serving as a detour for almost every blasted east-west highway on the continent, the Woodpecker coughed six times, spit up some greenish bile, flicked one last bit of black rubber into the air, and died.

We drained the gas line again, blew out the carb, and checked the sediment bulb, which did little more than renew the taste of sour gas we'd put in our mouths an hour or so earlier. Still she wouldn't start. Finally, in utter disgrace, we ran a chain from Lunchbox's pickup back to the tractor and drug her ignominiously to my shop. (And if you know anything about how these things go, you already know that the problem was that we ran out of gas. If we had splashed just another cup in her tank, we would have driven down the highway in triumph and glory. But no . . .)

Another THT, even more humiliation, but since it was done with a full complement of fellow tractorers and witnesses, the story lives on in various permutations at Eric's Tavern, and probably always will.

THIRD PARTY PURCHASES . . . AND YOU'RE NOT INVITED TO THE PARTY

Another friend, Dick Day (first time he ever came out here, I put his name on the calendar and couldn't get Linda calmed down for more than a week), once hauled tractors for me. That is, there is a THT in my life that I did in absentia. I don't recommend it. The other guys have all the fun, and there are some hazards inherent in letting someone else spend your money.

Or worse: I can't help but think of the story about the guy who buys some land, builds a cabin in the isolated wilder-nesses of, oh, say, Nebraska. One day a grizzled, tough, bat-tered guy appears at his door and announces that he is his neighbor from about 10 miles over the hills to the west.

He says, "I was wonderin' if you'd like to come over to my place for a little get-together tomorrow night. Drinkin', fightin', wild sex, that kind of thing." Well, the newcomer doesn't know much about local customs, so he asks, "Gosh, I guess so, but what should I wear to an occasion like this?"

"Doesn't matter," the old settler says. "Just gonna be you and me."

Actually, this tractor-hauling story I'm leading up to was a kind of double double-cross. Russ Meints lives in Corvallis, Oregon. He found out there was a John Deere B for sale here in Nebraska. Since he was going to be driving back from Virginia (or Delaware or South Carolina or one of those states with water, hills, and trees—they all look alike), he told me to buy this tractor for him and he'd just pick it up on his way through. Well, that sounds pretty simple, doesn't it? (MORAL: *Anytime anything sounds simple, get the hell away from it just as fast as you can, and that goes for love and romance and sex and marriage and tractors!*)

The B was about 75 miles away from my place, so I thought, gosh, why not ask my good buddy Dick Day to drop down and take a look at that tractor. It's not very far away from him. He can do the bargaining for me for Russ. (Notice the prepositions piling up. Not a good sign.) So, Dick did that. He gave me a kind of vague report on what he'd seen, because, well, actually, while he was there, he took along another friend who actually did the evaluations and conver-sation for Dick for me for Russ. I called Russ and told him what Dick's friend had told him to tell me to tell Russ.

Russ told me to tell Dick to tell his friend to tell the guy who owned the tractor that he would pay about half what he wanted, and we could see how that went down. So I told Dick to tell his friend to tell the owner what Russ had said. The guy told Dick's friend to tell Dick to tell me to tell Russ, okay, he'd sell for that price but without the wheels.

Now, it's always been my impression that a tractor without wheels offers some real problems, especially in loading and unloading, but the owner said, heck, he'd throw in delivery for just a little extra money, something like $100. Reasonable. That's what he told Dick's friend to tell Dick to tell me to tell Russ. And I did.

I sensed a certain air of complication developing here, but believe me, I had no idea what was in the works. Dick and his friend were to go back to the owner and make the deal and so that would be that. And now that pretty much settles things, right? I mean, jeez, the deal is nailed down, we bought the tractor, the guy is dropping it off, and Russ will be picking it up in a couple of weeks. The package is all wrapped and the bow is tied.

Uh huh. Yeah.

Dick went back there, all right, and he called me with the following report, pretty much verbatim:

"I got some good news for you. Really good news."

Uh-oh.

"I got the tractor for you for Russ."

"Uh-huh."

"And I got it for even less than he wanted to pay. Two hundred dollars less."

Uh-oh again. We had a rock-bottom price on this tractor as it was, without wheels, so what did it take, exactly, to cut that price in half?

"You probably wonder how I did that, and man, are you going to be proud of me."

This is getting worse by the minute.

"He didn't just have the one tractor."

Oh no. "You bought two tractors without wheels?"

"Uh, not exactly."

"Dick . . ."

"Actually, he didn't just have two tractors either."

"YOU BOUGHT THREE @#$%&*% TRACTORS?!"

"Well, not exactly, Rog."

He had bought four tractors, all John Deere Bs, all without carbs or mags, all without wheels to speak of. A couple of them wound up having what had been at one time, maybe 30 years ago, wheels, but no longer really wheels. Now, each tractor had a very good price on it, but we are now not looking at an arithmetic problem of 1 x good price = bargain. We are looking at 4 x good price, which looks a lot like 1 x really bad price = bad idea. Or, since these four tractors all together don't make up one decent machine, more like bad price x − 50 = total disaster.

Okay, we can talk about all this when Dick comes with the tractors, right? Well, no, not exactly. Dick won't be able to come by with the tractors. The seller and a friend of his will haul them here. Uh, okay, why wouldn't Dick want to come along with this shipment of antique treasures to collect the gratitude and affection of this friend of a friend for whom he bought the tractor(s)? You know perfectly well why.

At a prescribed time, okay, four hours after the prescribed time when it was totally dark, which made looking at the hulks a lot easier but unloading them a lot more difficult, the truck pulled into our yard. You wouldn't believe the barking, snarling, biting, and growling that ensued. And that

was Linda. The dogs retreated immediately to the safety of
their beds. They're no dummies. They wanted nothing to do
with what they saw in the yard.

Lunchbox, Woodrow, and I had been waiting four hours
for the delivery, and since it was a hot evening, we had gone
ahead and dived into the cooler I'd set up for the occasion.
And when it was empty, someone took another 20 of my dollars uptown and picked up another case. About that time the
guys with the tractors arrived, having also soothed their
fevered brows with several stops along the way.

Oh boy. Nothing like five drunks trying to unload four
total hulks of tons of jagged, cutting, slicing, grinding, filthy
steel from a truck bed in the dark. But my faith in the old
adage about God protecting drunks and fools proved well
founded: not a single one of us sustained any damage beyond
blurred vision and blitzed brain
cells through the next hours of
confusion, although Linda noted
later that there didn't seem to be
a lot of brain cells to begin with.

> I married beneath me. All women do.
> —NANCY, LADY ASTOR

I think her observation was something to the effect that it was
really interesting to watch five guys who all together didn't
quite make one complete quota of good sense unloading four
piles of iron that all together didn't quite make up one
decent tractor.

Women.

Probably the clearest sign of divine intervention involved
a slight problem we had with our unloading equipment. The
trailer, you see, had two loading ramps, but a JD B is a tri-
cycle arrangement; two big back wheels far apart and two
little front wheels real close together. The ramps would be
fine if we were hauling cars with four wheels or tractors with

wide front ends so the front wheels would track the same path as the real wheels. But noooooo . . .

Not that there was much by way of wheels to begin with, but still, the substantial weight of these things rested on three legs—two back wheels and one close pair in front. Even we could see that what we really needed was three unloading ramps.

To this day I cannot recall why we thought it would be a good idea, but for some reason, we half-rolled, half-dragged the rear-most tractor backwards to the back edge of the trailer, the alleged back wheels right on the brink of the two ramps. It may, actually, have been then that we first noticed we didn't have a middle ramp for the front pedestal. I think our plan was to sit down, have another cold one, and consider our problem. We may even have gotten that far.

Then something happened that, in a lot of other contexts, might have qualified as a bona fide miracle: This tractor, which we had every reason to believe was utterly incapable of rolling at all, rolled backwards. Maybe it was the tilt of the trailer bed, maybe it was the anticipation of that old tractor for its new home, maybe it was heavenly intervention. All I know is that all at once, before our amazed eyes, the rusted, bent, broken spokes of what had been wheels rolled just an inch or two backwards. Just enough to get them onto the ramps. With a terrible scream of iron against iron, bending twisting spokes, parting members, disintegrating rust, and the flapping of rotten rubber, that tractor started backwards down the ramps all by itself.

All five us agreed in the post-game debriefing that to our amazement, the one thing we all thought of was what was going to happen when the back wheels were on the ground and that front pedestal dropped 5 feet straight down to the drive, it having no ramp to roll down on. Would the lip of the trailer tear the front end off the tractor, or would the falling ton of tractor tear up the trailer? Would the pedestal shatter on hitting the ground? Bury itself so deep into the ground we would have to dig it out? Having never seen the front end of a tractor drop 5 feet straight down, not one of us had any idea how this 10th-of-a-second drama was going to be resolved.

Then the miracle happened, and to this day I cannot understand or explain it. At the very moment the big back wheels neared the bottom end of the ramps and the front of the tractor was at the trailer's edge, the shattered and bent spokes of what had been the right wheel caught in the steel mesh of the ramp. With a horrendous scream of twisting metal the wheel jammed, pivoting the front end of that wreck precisely so that the front pedestal arced right down the left ramp. There that tractor sat, flat on the ground.

We all agreed that, even stone sober, we couldn't have planned to back the tractor in such a way that the front pedestal would take the same path as one of the back wheels. Had that apparently dead machine, on its own, rescued itself from five bumbling human beings? Had a divine and merciful hand saved us from killing ourselves? I have no idea. All I know is that this is a true and honest account of exactly what happened.

I don't even remember how we got the other three tractors off that trailer. Doesn't matter.

You're thinking, well, that's a funny story. Rog bought four tractors for his buddy Russ. Not exactly. I bought two for me, or rather for Linda, who it turns out, has a sentimental thing for John Deere Bs, and two for Russ, who it turns out, comes into our yard a couple of weeks later with a new van he just bought somewhere in one of those states east of the Mississippi. He is not hauling a trailer to take his one/two tractor(s). No, he changed his mind. In the back end of his van he has two dismantled cars. (I am not exaggerating one little bit here, no matter how impossible this seems. Russ is a biology professor, and when I once visited him in his campus office I found that he had a totally dismantled Volkswagen bug lying about as if it were nothing more than discarded manuscript pages.) He not only wasn't going to take his two John Deere Bs on this trip, he wasn't going to take any John Deere Bs on this trip.

To this very day, more than two years later, all four of those ugly green hulks are still careened like wrecked pirate ships in our farmyard. Think I'm pissed? You should talk with Linda.

PATIENCE MAKES THE MECHANIC

Like most of my stories, there are a lot of morals to that one. But the most relevant to this weighty tome is that it really is true that given a lever and a fulcrum, an ordinary man could almost move the world. "Almost," because a fulcrum and a lever are darn useful, but you can move things along a lot more smoothly if you throw in a come-along winch and a couple of wedges, two or three rollers and a handyman jack, and a dang-near endless supply of log chains. I'd try to explain all that stuff, but as I will discuss in the chapter on resources, this is where you go to your Farm Boy Encyclopedia and ask the questions.

Before I moved dead tractors around, I moved buildings around. I participated in the moving of 10 buildings over a period of a few years. When asked to name my hobby for a human interest article in a local newspaper, I had no trouble in settling on "moving buildings." I moved five of them all by myself. I got pretty good at it.

The theory is the same as for breaking loose stuck parts on a tractor: take your time. I learned that much earlier when I climbed mountains. Early on I was surprised to find how much ground is covered with the mountaineer's step. Step, stop, step, stop, step, stop. It's about the best one can do without oxygen at high altitudes, and it works quite well. Same with breaking loose stuck motors: tap tap tap . . . douse parts with Liquid Wrench; tap tap tap . . . have a beer; douse parts with Liquid Wrench; tap tap tap.

That's how you move a house or shed or dead tractor, a half-inch at a time. You'll be surprised how soon that tractor is out of the swamp, forest, or collapsed barn and up onto your trailer. No special tools necessary. I went to a steel yard and got some short pieces of 4-, 6-, and 8-inch steel tube scraps between 4 and 18 inches long for rollers, but I've also had very good luck using round wooden fence posts. Enormous weights can be lifted with a plain old "handyman" farm jack, better yet, an old railroad jack if you can find one at a junkyard or farm auction.

If you don't know why a portable cable winch is called a "come-along," you can either try to hold back the cable while someone else operates the winch handle—a four-year-old girl will do fine—or stop by a farm when a calf is being pulled with a come-along.

It may seem slow, literally an inch or half-inch at a handle-pull, but before you know it, that tractor will be where you want it to be.

Within all this hoo-ha-ing, however, I just have to issue a stern warning about safety when doing this kind of thing. A snapped come-along cable, 2 tons of iron slipping off a jack, a foot or finger in the wrong place at the wrong time; there is always a potential for terrible disaster. No kidding. Wear gloves and boots, a safety helmet, and eye protection when doing this kind of stuff. Stay sober and focused on what you're doing. Or you may never get to enjoy whatever it is you're hauling off. Secure everything on ramps, rollers, or trailers with chocks and chains. It is stupid to climb mountains or move buildings or tractors without someone around to call the hospital when you hurt yourself. Yeah, I know I said I did it that way. That's how I know it's stupid.

At another time Dick Day offered to pick up an International Cub I bought near Lincoln, the one being unloaded by the recently divorced wife. I made a point of going with him on that buying expedition, and we came home with only one tractor. I'll never let anyone do a road trip without me, ever again.

CHAPTER 7

SHOP REPAIRS

(NOT THE TRACTOR—YOU!)

We don't know a millionth of 1 percent about anything.
—THOMAS ALVA EDISON

I like to think I'm a pretty tough guy. I'm 6 feet, 2 inches and weigh about 225 pounds. Okay, 240 . . . 250. But I absolutely despise anything to do with doctors. There's almost nothing they do in their offices that is any fun at all. Especially anything involving a needle. I recently had a heart catheterization in a hospital, mostly so far as I can tell because they had to figure out some way to pay for their new heart catheter.

Now, no matter what you've been told about the way to a man's heart being through his stomach, that's actually not the case. No, someone with a really perverse sense of humor figured out somewhere along the line that the way to run a little wire up to the heart is through an incision in your groin. Or worse yet, through *my* groin.

The only logic I can see behind this is that nurses pretty much spend their days dealing with sick and hurt people, crying babies, grouchy old farts, injury, disease, that kind of thing. As anyone can imagine, that sort of thing works on a person over time, so they cast around looking for something to bring a little cheer into their lives. Sort of like when a perfectly good dog left home too long with nothing to do decides it might be fun to eat a shoe or poop in the shower.

I am not suggesting for a moment that a nurse, who is probably someone's wife, maybe even a mother, seeks to deliberately inflict pain on some innocent like me when he comes along. No, during this recent experience I sensed nothing but care and concern on the part of the ladies in question.

Thing is, I like to do crossword puzzles. I've been doing them for 50 years now (crossword puzzles, not nurses), and I'm getting pretty good. The local newspaper publishes a Sunday puzzle that's pretty good, but it's still way too easy. So I make it tougher by starting with one word, and every word I add has to be attached from that point on to another word, sort of like Scrabble. And I use an ink pen. And I never consult a dictionary or the solution, if it is printed in the same paper. This makes it more interesting.

Same with nurses and patients. Sure, it would be easy enough just to cut a hole in a guy's chest and take a peek at what's going on in there, but how long is that going to hold your attention? Over time they work out other ways to do the job. Hey, on this one, let's feed a wire up to his heart from his crotch.

More than that, your average female nurse gets a kick out of shaving irregular patches on a man's chest. ("Hey, Louise, look at this! I shaved a happy face on this guy's belly! Let's paint his Family Pride with iodine and see what he does when he wakes up!") Without shaving cream or subtlety.

On this occasion, the nurse chatted cheerily with another, making sure to make plenty of eye contact, while taking long, quick swaths out of my thigh, belly, and chest hair with a double-edge razor. You know, right in the vicinity of things that have a long and natural aversion to sharp things. It was another nurse who pulled the lucky short straw for slathering alcohol on my raw skin with a mop.

In the movies, the medical personnel who do these chores on the handsome spy-hero of the story, fall hopelessly in lust with him at first sight, as it were. The ladies who did the dishonors during my particular and recent procedures were certainly pleasant and maybe even attractive, but in my condition—which is to say, scared, tired, sick, and drugged—I didn't much notice. Normally, I do notice such things.

Linda once splashed some toilet cleaner in her eye (which she says now exempts her from all further toilet-cleaning duties), and I had to rush her to a nearby emergency ward. It was a weekend and the usual doctors were off playing golf. The doctor on duty was, gulp, movie star gorgeous. I mean, this woman was the James Bond heart catheterizations shaver every man has in mind. Of course, first in my mind was the welfare and pain of my beloved wife, Linda. But well, you know, if Linda died of Drano poisoning, gosh, our daughter would need a good mother, and what could be a better mother than a doctor?!

This gorgeous creature was leading Linda into an examining room to flush her eyes, pausing only to turn to me and smile a warm, inviting smile. Our eyes met. I tried to express my gratitude to her with mine. (Yes, sure, I was grateful that she was caring for a loved one, but mostly I was grateful for her smile.) She turned back to Linda, to tell her what a prize she had in me, perhaps? To suggest a ménage à trois perhaps?

"If you want, Mrs. Welsch, your father can come along with you," she said.

And like a golden carriage at midnight, that miserable witch turned into a pumpkin, right there, on the spot.

Some tractors are like that. Nurses have a certain *je ne sais quoi* about them (that's French for "even harder to figure out than most women"), but the situations in which we encounter them have considerable effect on our final impressions. A tractor you may have fallen in love with at the auction and grown even closer to as you nursed it back to health in your shop loses a certain something the first time the crank snaps back and breaks your arm.

I later learned that accessing the heart by way of the inner thigh is neither a matter of amusement nor misanthropy. Hospitals, I was told, charge for this kind of work by the mile. With a long torsoed guy like me, any medical institution stands, therefore, to make a couple of extra bucks by going through the groin rather than, say, an armpit or nose. (The new fashion in vasectomies is to start in your ear, so you may want to watch out for that.)

Similarly, nurses may very well be paid for shaving duties by the acre, which would make the groin a better profit center than, say, the elbow, according to my medical expert, Eric, the bartender up at the tavern. But God bless the caretakers. They put up with a good deal more than any mechanic I know. When I go in for flu shots, instead of a sticker that says, "I'm a BIG BOY," I usually get one that says, "I PISSED AND MOANED." There have been times when the nurse was crying by the time she got done getting a needle in me.

I'm just not very good about such things, and it's not all my fault. I have what are called "rolling veins." When the time comes for a blood sample or a new IV (in the hospital, this will be about an hour after you have fallen asleep), it's like chasing that last piece of al dente spaghetti around an empty plate with a chopstick. The nurses dig and dig and dig with that square needle and try a new place and dig and dig some more. Yikes. Finally, in despair, after a nurse in Omaha spent nearly a quarter hour poking holes in me trying to pierce one of my radiator-hose veins, Linda sputtered to the nurse, "Just give him a butter knife, and in 15 minutes you'll have all the blood you need."

In fact, if you are at all like me, consider buying your Band-Aids by the pound, surgical tape by the reel, burn ointment by the tub, and disinfectant by the 6-gallon drum.

Personally, I would advise you to make one of the first things for a new shop a large, industrial-grade first-aid box in an obvious and easily accessible place. Put it above a flat surface where you can bleed without doing any real damage and apply medications and dressings with the undamaged hand, or in worst-case scenarios, your teeth.

Seriously, it shouldn't escape your attention, and it sure hasn't escaped mine, that a welding setup with an oxygen bottle is not a bad idea for an old guy with a cardiac history. (Be sure you suck on the right bottle in case of an emergency. I don't know, but I have a feeling acetylene might not have the same benefits as oxygen. I'm guessing it would generate an effect roughly similar to Linda's cabbage soup I love so much.)

GOOD MEDICINE

In other places I have touted the psychological, spiritual, and medical benefits of the hobbyist's shop work, and I would like to underscore that again here. I use the word *hobbyist* because I don't know how a real mechanic feels about his work. I can imagine that it is satisfying, sometimes even entertaining, but what we do for fun just isn't the same as what we do for work, a topic I have dealt with elsewhere in these pages. But I do know for a fact that the very first time I worked on an old tractor, and darn near every time since, whenever I've gone into my shop with a troubled mind, a weary body, a discouraged spirit, a stalled muse, I have come out renewed. Linda has seen that too and generously encourages me to take time out of the vexing parts of my life and indulge in the soothing therapy of my shop, even if it's just a little tinkering or cleaning up.

Maybe it's the throbbing rhythms of ZZ Top, or the smell of solvents and a wood-burning stove, or the glow of clean metal emerging from rust and grease. Maybe it's the inviting smiles of the naughty girls on my shop calendars. I don't know, but I know it's good for me.

I cannot for the life of me imagine why any woman would deny her man that kind of comfort, at least if she loves him. What could be more innocent than grinding a weld? What kind of threat to a relationship could deglazing a new piston sleeve possibly constitute? Yet this very week I received an e-mail message from a man turning to me for personal advice because his wife is getting huffy about the time he spends in the shop.

My first question of course was, "Well, how much time are you spending in the shop?" That is not so obvious an element as you might think. I once marveled when a good friend called me from Colorado and told me he had come home late from a rugby game in the next town to find that his wife had thrown out all his belongings onto the front lawn and changed the locks on the doors. This guy can be a real ass, but I was surprised because this couple had gone through so much together, things that might break up even the strongest of marriages. But here too I had the good sense to pursue the details just a touch further: "Uh, how late did you come back from that rugby game, Dave?" I asked.

"A week and a half," he answered.

Well, my correspondent of last week assured me that his shop time rarely amounted to two full days in the span of a month, and the shop is adjoined to his home. It's not as if he is boinking another woman on his deluxe creeper. The problem here, it seems to me, is not with the guy who wants to spend some time in his shop. It's with a woman who may not really care about the health and happiness of her husband, and that's not a pretty situation.

Okay, yeah, around here we joke a lot about our mènage à *soixante* (Linda, me, and 58 tractors), but I also know that Linda has actually accepted and paid for tractors delivered to our yard in my absence. It was she who shed tears when the beloved Woodpecker, heroine of the book *Busted Tractor and Rusty Knuckles*, was trailered out of our yard.

> *The only time a woman really succeeds in changing a man is when he's a baby.*
> **—NATALIE WOOD**

But you know, there are expectations from my public. Just as we are supposed to laugh about mothers-in-law, and I may remark about the wretched Lakota with three wives, all daughters of the same woman, my mother-in-law, Sally, is a perfectly wonderful woman and I love her. (In fact, since she is roughly my own age, I have often told my father-in-law that if things don't work out with Linda, well, gosh, I'd be interested in seeing Sally.)

So when my heart problems started last August, our first line of defense was humor, and most of all, tractor humor. For example, this time around (this was my second experience with atrial flutter, and I hope my last) I "flat-lined" for five or six seconds. They let me bring home the chart by way of a souvenir and reminder that it might be a good idea to slow down. Linda remarked almost immediately that was as quiet and cooperative as I had been in all the years since we first met 20 years ago. I noted that I was only "gone" for five seconds, but when I came to, Linda had already sold three of my tractors.

And here in town the story surfaced that three seconds into my momentary demise, Linda hot-footed it over to the local newspaper offices and asked how much it would cost to get my obituary published. "Two dollars a word," the guy behind the desk said, "But the first five words are free."

After only a moment's thought, Linda wrote down, "Rog died. Tractors for sale."

It's an apocryphal story, but it doesn't need to be. That is to say, it didn't really happen, but it sure could have. Linda's up to it. I once darn near killed myself in my shop with carbon monoxide. Really dumb. I started an engine up in a closed shop. Of course I know better! What do you think I am? Stupid? Okay, so I'm stupid. I figured I could run that engine for a minute or so without any real problems. Sure, carbon monoxide kills, but not like cyanide, right?

I don't know how long it was, but it wasn't long. I found myself starting to go down, and I knew what was happening. I lurched right straight, and with every ounce of determination in my body, toward the outside door. I was a trifle sick and pretty scared, so after catching my breath, dashing in to turn off that engine, and throwing open all the shop doors and windows, I went to the house and told Linda what had happened.

Being a woman, the first thing she wanted to do was call the doctor. Hey, I'm up, I'm alive, I've learned an important lesson. No need for my doctor, also a tractor mechanic, to diagnose my problem (terminal stupididiotosis). Being a real man, I ignored her instructions and went back out to the shop. Being a real woman, she ignored my instructions and called the doctor.

He told her I was probably all right, but that if I should "act goofy at all that evening," to give him another call. According to a later report from the doctor, she told him, "Rog acts goofy every evening."

There are lots of shop morals to that story:

1. NEVER start an engine in a closed shop.
2. Get a good carbon monoxide detector and hook it up. This is even more important than a burglar alarm in most shops.
3. Have someone check on you REGULARLY while you are working in the shop. There are way too many things that can go wrong and some timely help may save your life, even if it costs you some dignity.
4. Inform whomever that person is who checks in on you where your first-aid kit is and the kinds of things to look for. Pools of blood are obviously a crisis indicator, I know, but lying prone on your back under an engine transmission in a pool of oil is not, at least if the entire tractor is not resting on your prone body. (Linda, for example, has been instructed on how to open the valves on my welding setup's oxygen tank and the welding torch if it is hooked up. In the case of a stroke or heart attack, that little bit of shop knowledge could save my life, and I feel fairly strongly about that.)

COMFORT LEVELS CAN DIFFER

Linda is an artist, and she is always looking for models. Despite the generosity of Woodrow, Lunchbox, and even myself in offering to go to the Slammer, a local center for the, uh, interpretive dance, and check out some ladies who might be available for nude modeling, she insists on finding her own models, however. Linda doesn't spend any time in my shop, but I once suggested that she could come out there and do sketches of me while I worked. It didn't go well. Something about smoke, smell, noise, dirt, cursing, and blood put her off and she hasn't been back.

But it's not a matter of gender roles. There are women who love a good shop, and that's fine, but not very damn many. In fact, things have not gone well for Linda generally when she has attempted to cross the wide divide of Viva la Difference. I was once on a protracted speaking tour, and Linda decided to impinge on the male prerogative.

> *He's the kind of man a woman would have to marry to get rid of.*
> —MAE WEST

We live on a rough piece of ground with river frontage and tangled woods, so we constantly enjoy rich and varied wildlife. Which is to say, raccoons and opossums regularly raid and dismantle our garage, tearing open bags of dog and cat food, putting mud on our vehicles, busting up fishing equipment, and pooping with uncanny accuracy precisely where my feet fall on my way in and out of the building.

I suppose we've hauled 30 or 40 coons and opossums out of this place in the last four months, taken them 5 or 6 miles to a local wildlife refuge, and turned them loose. It then takes them, we figure, the better part of a week to get back here and go back to work again. I don't even have to bait the live trap anymore: They just go in and flip the trigger because they have come to enjoy the ride in the pickup truck so much.

So, I was working some place out of town, probably in the Degenerate East—Omaha or Des Moines—and a raccoon was still raising 53 brands of hell with our garage nightly. Linda decided to set the trap herself. That's the easy part. Checking it in the morning isn't all that tough either, but I don't think Linda gave a full dose of thought to what would happen if she actually caught something.

Neither did I. In fact, I even encouraged her. See, for weeks I'd been catching what I presumed to be members of the same raccoon family. They were all about the same size. Maybe a year old, real timid, cute, and cuddly. I have often wanted to cook up a raccoon stew, mostly just to say I did, but I guess I'll have to watch for a road kill because I don't think I'll ever be able to bring myself to shoot one of these cute rascals.

So I told Linda over the phone, when she told me her plans, "Yeah, go ahead. You've seen me set the trap. You can do it. And if you do catch one of those cute little bandits, just throw him into the back of the truck and run him out to the game reserve. Or call one of my buddies and have him do it for you."

God, the innocence in that sort of confidence! I called Linda the next morning about 7 A.M. before I set off on the highways to my next speaking engagement. It was a little early, but she usually gets up to get Antonia off to school. Well, she was up all right. In fact, she'd been up since 3 A.M. and had been to the emergency ward and back already.

As she tells the story, she woke up about 3 A.M. with all hell breaking loose in our yard. The dogs were going crazy, and as far as she could tell, 30 or 40 black bears were holding a wrestling tournament out in the garage. She threw on a robe and went out to see what was going on. Now, that poses some uneasiness even in me. I dread the morning I go out there and find I have cleverly trapped, for example, a skunk. Well, Linda's catch of the day was not one of the cute lil' rascals I'd been hauling off. She caught their mommy, and she wasn't amused in the least by the inconvenience this had injected into her schedule.

What's worse, Linda didn't understand and I failed to explain that a raccoon in a live trap wants out pretty bad and reaches for every conceivable possible tool that might affect an escape. And boy, can a big raccoon reach! That coon sow had grabbed and dragged into our live trap newspapers, cans, tools, plastic, gravel, and most of my fishing equipment. Line, weights, and bait, most of which she had also eaten, quickly digested, and redistributed about the trap. And before Linda could drag that live trap, now full of a very large and very angry raccoon, away from her entangling alliances, she had to fish, you should pardon the expression, some of the junk away from the trap.

She took off the gloves she had wisely donned for this filthy and risky chore and reached down to pull away a corrugated worm, a plastic lure one dips into stink bait when angling for catfish. (If I get around to it, I'll tell you more about stink bait later. It really does have something to do with tractors.) Just as she daintily grasped it, the coon lunged angrily toward her hand. Linda quite understandably jerked her hand back. Burying the treble hook deep into her right forefinger. On one hand, it was good the lure was brand new and clean; on the other hand, as it were, that treble hook was also new and razor sharp.

So instead of calling Mel and Sue Halsey at, oh, 9 A.M. to help her haul the raccoon away, she called them at 4 A.M. to get her to the emergency ward to remove the hook. There's a lot more to the story, but the main thing is, while Linda was being admitted to the hospital, the nurse asked her, "Are you married?"

"Up till now," she said.

Some sharing of marital duties can strengthen a healthy relationship. Some don't. Take it from me: Some don't.

CHAPTER 8

KIDS, DOGS, MUSEUMS, FARMS, AND BEER

(BEING THE PHILOSOPHY, THEOLOGY, AND FOOLOLOGY OF TRACTOR RESTORATION)

Ah, the devil's in the women, and they never can go easy.
—IRISH FOLKSONG

A shop is probably not the best place for a toddler. My father never thought it was the best place for a grown son. Mostly it was that matter of me borrowing tools and never bringing them back, I think. Antonia used to come out in my shop and even helped me clean parts and scrape engines; but then she was out there once when a photographer from *Successful Farming* magazine came by and shot some photographs for my column in that splendid magazine. The photo was published, father and daughter, grinning side by side, scrapers in hand, draped in filthy shop aprons. I was a very proud papa.

Antonia never came out to the shop again. It may have been comments from her peers at school because she had, in this photo, inadvertently admitted to having a parent, something no self-respecting teenager would ever do, but I think it was more a matter of plain old human nature. Or woman nature, at least. All I need to do to fritz any kind of deal with Antonia is to tell her what it is I would like, and I can be absolutely confident that she will do precisely the opposite. She is at this very moment considering where she will go for her higher education. There are a lot of schools I cannot possibly afford, so I have to be very careful not to tell her which ones they are, because if I do, that is precisely where she'll want to go.

I have known this for quite a while, having successfully negotiated the minefield of bringing three other children to adulthood, if not always maturity. It is the nature of living creatures to be contrary. Being a Czech Catholic, Linda thinks it's a matter of being a German Lutheran, me being a German Lutheran. I have been, I think, remarkably generous in throwing out my idea for making anyone a millionaire almost instantly: Develop a dog food called "The Other Dog's Food" or a toy (it doesn't really matter what it is) dubbed "The Other Kid's Toy." That is precisely what dogs and children want—and most humans and even other creatures, from oysters to eagles. What we want is first of all, most of all, what the other guy has.

This isn't always bad. In fact, it can be as useful as a 9/16ths combination wrench. My pal Woodrow is a pretty savvy country boy. Not all that educated, but not all educated people are savvy either. Sometimes, however, even Woodrow surprises me with his understanding of things, whether it's tractor mechanicking, the ways of women, or the nature of children.

Not long ago I went fishing with Woodrow, and once we had our lines thrown out, he pulled a wad of paper out of his pocket, stuck it toward me with a grin, and said, "Take a look at this." The paper had been hauled in and out of his pocket so often, it was beaten into a paper-towel consistency. I unrolled it, presuming it was another of those things men share in taverns and on fishing trips, bits of obscenity and pornography that have been photocopied so often they're scarcely legible any longer. And usually not all that funny.

I was, therefore, a little surprised to find that what I had was a bunch of notes and letters from teachers and administrators of the school our children attend. It wasn't the source of the notes that surprised me, actually. I had seen an endless parade of notes on this same letterhead, sent to Woodrow about one of his children, Benson, whom he described variously as "high-spirited," "under-challenged," "mischievous," or "that little bastard who can't seem to do anything without getting into trouble."

People locked their doors when they saw Benson in the streets and locked their children, dogs and cats in the garage. Then they dialed the first six numbers of the sheriff's office just to get a head start on the call they would almost certainly have to make when Benson decided exactly where to turn his attention on this fine day. These papers I was holding were all labeled with the name *Benson*. Same as usual.

The surprise was in Woodrow's smile, and the unlikely— no, impossible—contents of the first note I read. And of the next. And the next and the next and the next and the next. "Benson has made a remarkable turn for the better in his work this semester." "Benson's grades are the top in his class." "Benson has turned his grades around." "I wish every student was like Benson." "Benson's attitude is exemplary."

I looked at Woodrow utterly flummoxed. He grinned back. I handed him the papers. He tucked them proudly back into this pocket, ready to be paraded before the next person he could corner into looking at them.

"What . . .?" I asked.

Since he'd been asked the same question by the previous 336 people he'd shown the papers to, he didn't need to hear the rest. "Benson was bit by a sewer snake," he explained.

Again, I didn't have to ask. I looked at him until he thought I'd rolled his response around in my mind for a suitable period, and then he explained. Last year when Benson was expelled from school, precisely as he'd been expelled every previous year, Woodrow took a new tack with the lad. He made him his on-the-job assistant.

> Women speak two languages, one of which is verbal.
> —STEVE RUBENSTEIN

Woodrow is a plumber. He says there are only three things you need to know to be a plumber: (1) Shit runs downhill, (2) don't bite your fingernails after working on a sewer line, and (3) payday is Friday. I like Woodrow and he is a good storyteller, but there are a lot of his stories I'd just as soon not hear again. Especially his plumbing stories, adventures in the crawl spaces under mobile homes, interesting and unusual things clogging toilets, that sort of thing.

For the 10 weeks Benson was his assistant, Woodrow never turned down a plumbing job, no matter how disgusting. Whatever the job, Woodrow never failed to assign the very worst dimensions of it to his new assistant. Woodrow was smart enough not to couch this exercise in the form of punishment. No, he proudly took Benson to his bosom and told him and everyone else within hearing that Benson was his assistant, and he expressed his immense pride that the boy was following in his father's footsteps, taking up the noble trade, honored since the days of the Romans.

Benson is his father's son, and no dummy either. He had a choice and he made it wisely. He became an honor student. I am urging Woodrow to go somewhere with this now that Benson has graduated, a kind of Woodrow Barnaby Wilson Educational Fellowship Program. (I've already reserved a spot in Woodrow's graduate program next summer for Antonia.)

THE RELIGION OF WRENCHING

It's human nature, and I think that's a lot of what this whole business of mechanicking, restoring, collecting, and generally loving old tractors is all about. Thing is, very few of us have to work on old tractors. That's why it's fun. I can always amuse Al Schmitt, our local mechanic, by pulling into his place on a Friday afternoon, and when he says he's looking forward to a two-day vacation from his shop, tools, and balky vehicles, I express my own anticipation of a two-day vacation in my shop, with my tools, working on balky vehicles.

But it is, I've come to think, an even grander issue, because if it was just a matter of doing something different, would we (those of us who love and work on old tractors) simply, well, do something different? Work on, say, window fans? Or play in pinochle tournaments? Or sort salt and pepper shakers? No, the passion here is too strong and too deep for this simply to be a matter of a different direction or killing time.

Now, listen up close because I'm going to get serious on you here for a minute. And for those of you who finished high school, try to stay awake. In physics there's some sort of law or rule or notion to the effect that for every action there is an opposite and equal reaction. I think anthropologists might want to take a look at that idea too.

For example, I like good beer. Not long ago, right after my cardiac problems, I walked into Eric's Tavern up in town and, following the good doctor's orders, told him I wanted something with "no sodium, no sugar, no caffeine, no alcohol; no solids, no color, no taste, no interest." "Well," he said, "that leaves out Dannebrog water," and he popped open a Coors Lite for me. Which is to say, when I say "good beer," I'm pretty much leaving out American beer.

Most of my life I have preferred imported beers. I usually explain that I like Heineken or Saint Pauli Girl, Labatt Blue, or Moosehead because they are made in areas of the world plagued with an excess of water. I am, therefore, doing my part to balance God's mistake, a participant in Divine Intervention, not to mention meeting my obligation to the World Community, by taking water from places where they don't need it and putting it here, in my backyard, where we DO need it.

What's more, that water percolates through the sand of this miserable sack of gravel I call a farm, into the nearby Loup River, into the Platte, and down the Missouri. Irrigating crops all along the way, driving electric turbines, floating barges of grain, stone, automobiles, and cattle to ports throughout this country, and thence to New Orleans and on to other parts of the world that are hungry for nutritious food, reliable transportation, and building materials. That's why I drink imported beer.

It's also better beer. I know that one's choice of beer is to some degree a matter of taste. That is to say, I like taste; but this is my book so I get to say whatever I want to.

Ten years ago I cursed and puled as I watched Budweiser and Miller crush every small brewery across the nation, at each

eradication taking another variation out of our taste reper-
toire. It got to the point where I'd drink dreadful beer—
Hanley's, Blatz ("The beer as good as its name"), Bavarian
Club, even Plain Label—just to get a different taste. I imagined
and feared the day when there would be two choices of
American beer and absolutely nothing else. Maybe even just
one. I actually like Miller and Bud—they're certainly not Coors
Lite. It's just that I resented the loss of variety and choice.

That situation is mercifully changing. It already has
changed. I'll bet there are more small breweries in America
today than there were 30 years ago, in fact. It seems like every
little town has its own microbrewery, producing very small
quantities of beer, sometimes bad beer, sometimes good beer,
sometimes interesting beer, but never boring beer. I don't
think those two movements (bigger and bigger breweries, and
all at once more and more little breweries) are coincidental. I
think there are more and more little breweries because for a
while, there were fewer and fewer, bigger and bigger breweries.

It's not just commerce and economics. It's human
nature.

THE RIGHT FIT

Another case in point: farms. Thirty years ago I was
brought in as a consultant to a new-concept museum outside
Des Moines, Iowa, the now famous (and darn near midtown)
Living History Farms. They had a pretty good start and plan for
reconstructing their farm of the early 1800s and were making
even better progress with the farm of 1900 (because they pretty much started with a farm that had been built around 1900,
and it's easier to do research in agriculture of 70 years ago
than 150 years ago). The problem they faced at the moment
was what to do for a farm of the future (which, I laugh and cry

to tell you now, was to be the farm of 2000!). Would farms in that far distant time be high-tech, petrochemically based industrial operations with gigantic equipment and little human involvement or or or, well, what? And we were sitting around brainstorming, which is to say, guessing.

I came up with what to this day I consider the perfect solution (which the folks at the Living History Farms have understandably and just as insistently ignored). I recommended that visitors, after passing through the farms for 1820 and 1900, should be guided along a path that then split into two alternative farms for 2000, Farm of 2000 A and Farm of 2000 B. Farm of 2000 A would be what the ag and industry people projected, that high-tech, petrochemical, industrial farm of science fiction; Farm of 2000 B would lead museum visitors back to the farm of 1820.

I think it would not only have been a good story, and a fair warning, but maybe even an accurate prediction. It's not happening quite that way, no oxen, horse-drawn equipment, hand planting and harvest, log houses, all that. But around here, just as some farms and ranches are becoming ever bigger, gobbling up little farmers and ranchers around them, mining the soil for every last dollar that can be squeezed out of it, there is that opposite and equal reaction. More and more, smaller and smaller plots and parcels, owned by people like me, who don't need to take anything more than pleasure and surplus from the soil and water.

That sort of phenomenon is a matter of commerce and economics in a strategic, long-term sense, but not in the tactical, immediate vision most real business people seem to be embracing these days. I think that's what's going on with some of us, maybe most of us, who work on and love old tractors. While there certainly is a wonderful romance of working with old iron that I've waxed poetical about in other books (usually to the utter disbelief and ridicule of real mechanics, I should add), a sense of preserving the past, remembering, passing along memories, honoring ancestors, all that, I think there is also an element—a neglected element—of the collector-restorer-enthusiast speaking to the future.

Isn't there almost always a reaction from those who visit our shops, shows, exhibits, museums, and parades, or who read our publications, or see us along the roads, or read our books—an element of wonder for the wonderful and even beautiful efficiency, reliability, strength, beauty, and durability of our ancient machines? Just a touch of sometimes explicit envy and regret that we don't have those sorts of things around us today. And, get ready, here it comes: a hope that a day will come when we have things like that around us again.

I was once sent by a government agency to interview an old gent who shook me to my foundations with this kind of strategy. We stood in his barn as he absent-mindedly brushed at one of his big draft horses, who occasionally and appreciatively turned a massive head back to

He'd argue with a compass.
—DAVE RATLIFF

nudge the old gent. This guy had gone to the banker a few years before and asked for a substantial loan to buy some new, more advanced farming equipment, update and repair others, that kind of thing.

For those of you not familiar with farming these days, a big tractor costs more than $100,000, maybe even $200,000. Start with that tractor and begin adding other items: $50,000 pickup truck, a $120,000 combine maybe, some grain haulers, augurs, plows, listers. . . . It doesn't take long to build up a million dollars of debt, and more in annual debt interest than a lot of us make as total income.

It was hard times in both farming and banking, the banker explained, and this farmer was approaching old age. Sure he was in good condition and had always been a good farmer, but even good men and good farmers go down in cruel economies like America's. With little family and no children to assume the debt should something happen to the old man, well, there just couldn't be any loans this year.

"But all I've done all my life is farm. What am I supposed to do?" the farmer asked. The banker had no answer other than no.

The old gent went home, pretty beat down, but that night he had an inspiration. The next day he toured the farms of local friends, and some salvage yards, and bought up a mess of old tack and horse-drawn equipment for next to nothing, all of it so simple even a doofus like me could figure it out and repair it. And he bought himself a pair of good draft horses (and later a second team). He got rid of all the land he was renting, sold off all his own land holdings but what he thought he could handle with that team, and he went back 50 years in time.

He told me, and I believed him, that with absolutely no debt to service, pretty much growing his own fuel (and fertilizer!) he was realizing profits at least equal to what he was making before, and in some years well beyond what he earned during his years of frantic, industrial farming. But again, this was not for him simply a matter of economics and commerce, and I believed him about that too.

> *I could now afford all the things I never had as a kid, if I didn't have kids.*
> —ROBERT ORBEN

He patted his horse lovingly and told me that for years he'd been coming out to this same shed with dread and anger, crawling once again into the cab of a gigantic and complex tractor that was killing him financially, first for payments and then for repairs. But now, he smiled, he came out in the morning and Pat and Mike helped him meet the new day with warmth and good cheer. He said that he found in fields he had owned and farmed for decades a new joy and beauty. Smells and colors he'd forgotten, peace and comfort he never found in the cab of an air-conditioned high power tractor or combine. And I believed him.

I asked him what his neighbors thought and said about his gigantic step backwards. He laughed and said I'd just summed it up pretty well. They saw him as an old and crazy coot trying to relive the past. He said there wasn't the least doubt in his mind that he had actually made one, maybe even two, gigantic steps forward. No matter how much his neighbors wondered how he could conceivably farm like that intellectually yet economically, their bewilderment could never match his in his amazement that they could conceivably farm the way they were. The way he used to.

Boy, did I believe him.

I wonder if there isn't a bit of that in what we are doing, we old-tractor nuts. Maybe accidentally, but it's there. I've never heard anyone say something like "I am restoring/collecting these tractors because I want to preserve and propose for the future the potential of an alternative technology." But I once asked Mr. Fool Bull if he was passing along any of his encyclopedic knowledge of plant medicines to someone young, and he said no. I expressed my concern and disappointment because it would certainly be a shame if all this knowledge were lost.

Mr. Fool Bull laughed and explained that if we somehow forgot that aspirin helps alleviate headaches, it wouldn't mean that aspirin no longer alleviated headaches. It would only mean that somewhere, somehow we would have to learn again that aspirin alleviates headaches, and maybe we would learn it yet once again from chewing on a willow stick and noting that the salicin of the willow's inner bark metabolizes to salicylic acid—aspirin, which alleviates headaches.

Same with old tractors. Just because we don't know precisely what is going on here in our own minds, it doesn't mean something isn't still going on.

CHUGGING ALONG

On various occasions that Linda remembers with uncanny accuracy, I have gambled, uh, invested in the stock market. I have learned one thing for sure from those misadventures: The stock market has nothing to do with anything. You can do all the research you want; doesn't mean a thing. Get a hot tip under the table from the CEO? Doesn't mean a thing. A sure sign from God, maybe? Clouds in the sky directly over your head reading quite clearly, "Put everything you have into IBM"? Nothing.

When Antonia was just a child, she announced that she wanted to grow up to own a Toys R Us store. "By golly, Little One," I enthused in my best Daddy Warbucks tones, "This is America! You can own Toys R Us right now!" I opened the newspaper to the market reports and showed her Toys R Us, right there, on the New York Stock Exchange, and for $46 a share, she could own some. I showed her on my computer how the stock had steadily climbed for years, much better than the savings she had in a passbook account in the local bank. A good lesson in economics and investment, I thought.

It turned out to be a better lesson than I could ever have hoped for. That was many years ago and Toys R Us stock has never been back up to $46 a share. In fact, it has never been back up to $26 a share. The very day I bought the stuff with her money was the 20-year high for the stock.

But the real point is, you can't get rich planning to get rich. At least not me. Money just doesn't seem to have much to do with me, but there are other rewards in which I truly am rich, not the least of which is the satisfaction I get from working on (oh, let's be honest!) *playing* with my tractors. One of the reasons I left teaching is that more and more young people were asking really stupid questions about classes and education like "How is this going to make me any money?"

"How the hell would I know how it's going to make you any money?!" I would answer. "Education isn't about money. Education will make you an educated person. Maybe nothing will make you a rich person. Maybe something you would never have expected will make you rich." A lot of people, including me, ridicule those, among them Linda, who buy lottery tickets. "A tax on stupidity," we call it. And yet the fact of the matter is, all life is a craps shoot, a roll of the dice. Who would have thought that through a series of really dumb, okay, stupid accidents, coincidences, mistakes, and bullheadedness I would have wound up a friend of Charles Kuralt and eventually have a regular slot on his *CBS Sunday Morning* show for 12 years? Certainly not me, or anyone I know.

Who would have predicted the first time I ever twisted a wrench on a tractor, at the age of 55 (having never before so much as changed the oil in a car), I would fall utterly in love with the notion? And write books about it? And that you would

be reading it? Planning how to make money at working at tractors, or doing anything else, is like having a system for beating
the lottery.

The real reason for doing such things is because they're
fun. That's enough of a reason.

You know, I think there's something to that romantic
nonsense in mechanicking too. I know a good mechanic
knows an awful lot of hard, solid, no-nonsense facts. I know
the lessons are sometimes in classes, sometimes from publications, sometimes from masters in the field, and sometimes
from experience. But I also know that the last time I watched
one of the best mechanics I know, good ol' Melvin Nelson,
check over a troubled tractor engine, he ran his hands over it
and felt it. Pretty much like a high-priced doctor checking a
child for symptoms: "Does it hurt here? Cough. Breathe
deep and hold your breath. Any funny feelings here?" And
the only way Melvin could understand the responses from
that tractor is to know its language and soul. I don't think you
can get that from a classroom teacher or a book.

CHAPTER 9

TRACTORS AND THE ARTS

There is a new awareness of style in the Soviet Union. The premier's wife recently appeared on the cover of House and Tractor.

—JOHNNY CARSON

L ovely Linda has an art studio. In it she struggles with mechanical, aesthetic, and intellectual problems. She comes out of it smudged with paint, plaster, and dust. Her studio smells of paint, turpentine, and varnish. In it she creates things of timeless beauty. She is an artist, and what she creates is art.

I have a shop. In it I struggle with mechanical, aesthetic, and intellectual problems. I come out of it smudged with grease, dirt, and blood. My shop smells of gasoline, old rubber, sweat, and a dead mouse. In it I restore things of timeless beauty. I am a nuisance, and what I create is loud.

There you have it: Linda is an artist. I am not. That is sort of like saying, "Claudia Schiffer is quite attractive; Marge Schott isn't." You simply cannot imagine how much Linda is an artist, and you simply cannot imagine how much I am not. When Linda draws something, it not only looks like what she's drawing, it really looks like what she's drawing, to the point where it looks more like what she's drawing than the thing she's drawing looks like what she's drawing.

Me, on the other hand . . . My first encounter with art was when I was just turning four. My folks bought me a chalkboard. (At least I didn't have to write on a shovel by firelight.) Being my folks, however, they didn't buy me any chalk. Dad told me, "Just go outside and find some chalk." I cannot to this day imagine why he thought he could send a four-year-old kid out into the streets of Lincoln, Nebraska, and he would find some chalk lying around. There aren't even any rocks in Lincoln, Nebraska, let alone chalk.

Dad certainly had never found any chalk lying around in Lincoln, Nebraska, because geologists have never found chalk lying around in Lincoln, Nebraska. Neither had any human being in the entire history of the state, or prehistory, because not even Indians had found chalk where there would eventually spring the Star City of Lincoln, Nebraska. But my dad sent me out to find some chalk, in Lincoln, Nebraska.

I didn't even know what chalk was or what it looked like. So Dad described it to me, and did it quite well I should note. (I'm giving the Old Man the benefit of the doubt here.) Well, I almost immediately found what I presumed to be chalk and took it home. Unfortunately, it turned out to be a well-weathered dog turd. (Dog turds used to turn white in the olden days. I have no idea why they no longer do that. Or maybe the white ones are all picked up by kids sent out by cruel parents to pick up chalk, but that's not the point of this story.)

My view of the arts has been pretty much determined by that first experience. The very first day in kindergarten at Saratoga Public School, the teacher, Miss Farquhar, thinking she was making things easy for us, told us all to take a crayon and draw a picture. To my knowledge, up to that point in my life I had never so much as held a crayon in my fingers without eating it, and the idea of "drawing a picture" had never occurred to me. So I did pretty much what I have done the rest of my life when confronted by this kind of challenge: I started blubbering. Miss Farquhar took me to her warm, ample bosom and brushed away my tears (which probably explains why all my romantic adventures later in life fell pretty much into the category of "Worthy of Pity").

Miss Farquhar told me (God, I can remember this traumatic moment right now, 60 years later, as if it were yesterday) just to take a blue crayon for the sky above and green for the grass below, and make a picture of what I

> *Love is what happens to men and women who don't know each other.*
> —W. SOMERSET MAUGHAM

could see out the school window. My mother still has to this day the pathetic product of my artistic efforts that day: a now-crispy and yellowed sheet of school art paper with a blue line across the top and a green line across the bottom. (I suppose, now that I look back on it, I should have known something was wrong when it took the other kids so much longer to make their pictures.)

Now, consider Linda again a moment: She was once explaining "contour drawing" to me. In an effort to show me that art is not so much in drawing outlines as it is of capturing the spirit of the model, she took a large piece of paper, put her pencil down on it, and looked at our dog, Slump, asleep on the front room floor. Without ever lifting her pencil from the paper or looking away from the dog (or at the paper!) she moved that pencil in one steady, wiggly line. A couple of minutes later she lifted the pencil and said, "There," and sure enough, there on that paper was a drawing of Slump. Not just a bunch of lines that might be loosely interpreted as a dog, but Slump. It was like a miracle, and frankly, I still think it was.

To this day I walk into her studio with awe. My first word in this chapel is always "Wow!" I still tend to believe artists should stick to painting naked women and dogs playing cards, but I also know that this school of art theory is pretty much out of favor these days. We don't have that many dogs anyway, and Linda has always been rather stuffy about naked women sitting around here.

When Linda was taking art classes at the university, before we were married, she was always bringing around her work and quite a few of them were of coed models, nekkid as a jaybird. While I enjoyed her drawings, plenty, I thought I should share more of Linda's interests and maybe, uh, just drop by one of her evening classes sometime and see the creative spirit in process. I managed somehow to say that with a straight face, and she agreed I could come to her class that very evening. Oh boy, nekkid girls and I wouldn't even have to stuff dollar bills in the tops of their socks!

It was with substantial expectation that evening that I drove to campus, found the building and then the room where she told me her painting class would be meeting. I walked in, trying just as hard as I could be to look like someone really, really interested in art, and without the slightest inclination to look at, oh, say, boobs. I tried not to sweat. Or drool.

I didn't even look at the model when I walked in. I said to myself, "Self, play it cool." Linda came to me the moment I entered the door and led me to her easel. I looked at the painting, and then up—oh boy—to the model.

HOLY COW! THE MODEL WAS A MAN! AND HE WAS NEKKID AS A JAYBIRD!

And he didn't have his back turned to Linda, if you catch my drift here. And if he had swiveled too fast, he would've knocked down all the easels in the front row. And there was my future bride, Linda, not just looking at this mule standing there in all his glory (and nothing else), but she was looking at him real close. And of course about the time I got there, she was in the very process of painting his, well, I'd say privates, but what this guy had was more like commissioned officers than privates, and maybe even generals. And she was painting them in depressingly accurate detail, looking first at the subject and then at the canvas, back to the subject, down to the canvas, back to the subject, and on and on and on.

First I had to find my own chalk, then I had to draw a picture with crayons rather than eating them, and now this. Art has not been kind to me.

FINDING A FORTE

I've recovered. I don't draw or paint pictures, but I think I can say in all honesty and confidence that I have in my dotage become something of an artist. And it all happened in my shop, while working on a tractor.

Tractors themselves are gloriously artistic. Why are there not more classic paintings of tractors by the masters, you ask me—Renoir, Rembrandt, Degas, Monet? Well, mostly because there weren't any tractors when they were painting, but beyond that, well, think about it. You are an artist and you can either paint a picture of a naked woman or a Rumely Oil-Pull. You decide to paint a . . . ? I rest my case.

And yet, within a few miles of where I am sitting this very moment, there are probably 10 farmsteads where ancient, disabled tractors and miscellaneous, obsolete farm machinery have been artistically arranged as lawn ornaments. Most of the time they are painted up fancy, but in some cases they are simply rusted hulks. They sit in little flowerbeds, sometimes on a rock or concrete bed. They are clearly and deliberately positioned so they can be seen—and appreciated—by passersby. Isn't this pretty much what art is about? (And, while I don't know a lot about Mrs. Renoir, Mrs. Rembrandt, Mrs. Degas, or Mrs. Monet, I have a feeling even they would've been fussy about putting a naked woman out there. And yikes, I don't even want to think about the neighbor ladies and a naked woman, yet the naked woman and Nebraska winters!)

A few years ago I took up welding with the intention of eventually getting into some basic bodywork on my tractors. Up to then, and really up until now, my joy has been taking wrecked, stuck, discarded tractors and getting them running and rolling again. I haven't cared what they look like, but I thought maybe I could at least get to a point where I could weld broken fuel or choke controls, maybe even fender tears, pound out some dents, that kind of thing. Maybe even some painting.

I have done some of that. I am most proud of an air cleaner whose rusted-out bowl I braised (and darn near every Allis air cleaner bowl is rusted out, I have since found) and painted. It looked really good, considering it was me who did it. And I've done some passable welding. But last year I was working on a WC that I really wanted to do a good job on; in fact, I'm still working on it. But the problem was, no matter how good a job I did on everything else, the thorn on the rose, so to speak, was the really rough and ugly steering wheel. The rubber had cracked and most of it was broken off. It was even going to be tough to drive this thing out of the shop without tearing up my hands, it was clear.

When my interest in old tractors first sprang up, I had the incredible good fortune of attending one of the Goodyear-sponsored restoration workshops, offered at the time by the master restoration father-son team of Carroll "Oppy" and son Jeff Gravert. (I later, with glee, learned that these world-class tractor restorers lived in Central City, just down Ormsby Road from my place!) In my notes, I found that they'd suggested using an epoxy named PC-7 for restoring damaged steering wheels, and I decided to give it a try.

PC-7 is not easy to find (I finally found some at the Ace Hardware store in Grand Island, Nebraska). It comes in small tins and as far as I can tell isn't available in more economical quantities and is painfully expensive. I told Linda I got it to repair things around the house, which is pretty true. Mostly. But I was also thinking about giving a try at rebuilding that shattered steering wheel.

My uneasiness in starting this project did not result exclusively from my previous, painful experiences with art. I had, in fact, tried one previous steering wheel restoration early in my tractor-rebuilding career, using Bondo auto body repair epoxy. The experience with Bondo was a disaster: It sets up way too fast for this kind of work, and freezes into great, jagged globs on the steering wheel frame. Downright dangerous for a doof like me.

Dear Sweetheart:
Last night I thought of you.
At least I think it was you.
—LOVE LETTER
BY SNOOPY
(CHARLES SCHULTZ)

I cleaned the metal frame of the steering wheel with compressed air and wire brushes, picked off loose pieces of the old rubber, blew off and brushed the remaining rubber carefully, and blew out all the cracks and crevices. (I saved larger pieces of the old rubber that I thought were too loose to leave on the frame because I thought, even unattached, they might help me maintain the profile of the original rubber as I worked the PC-7 around the wheel. But then as Linda will tell you, I never throw anything away.)

PC-7 comes in two cans, one kind of light gray (I suspect there is a fancy name for the color. You know, Venetian mauve or burnt eunuch or something like that, but I'll leave that kind of thing up to smart-alecky artists) and the other black (or "pitch black"). You take two gobs of each, as equal as possible, and mix them together.

There are some important things you need to know about this part of the process:

Really do try to get equal amounts of the two parts; if you use too much of one or the other you may find the stuff won't set up properly. When I made this mistake on a couple of occasions, I found that by putting the wheel closer to the wood stove overnight where it was warm, the chemical reaction of the PC-7 was accelerated and it did eventually set up. (And that's what this is, a chemical reaction. It isn't a matter of "drying.")

Don't mix up too much at one time. PC-7 is much slower than Bondo, but the stuff is so expensive, you really don't want to wind up mixing quantities you'll only have to throw away. Since I wanted to be careful with the steering wheel and make it look good, I didn't want to hurry anyway.

Do your mixing on a clear surface with a clean mixing stick. I use old credit cards. We get three or four unsolicited credit cards a day around here, and as Linda will tell you, well, you know already, I never throw anything away. I use a whole card for the plate I mix the stuff on, and I cut up another card into four or five long strips for stirring sticks. CAUTION: NEVER USE THE SAME IMPLEMENT TO DIG A WAD

OUT OF ONE CAN AND THEN THE OTHER!! If you do something this dumb, you will mess up both cans and waste a lot of PC-7, not to mention money. Use two separate strips of credit card for this part of the operation, one for the black goo, the other for the gray goo.

I then use another piece of credit card to apply the now thoroughly mixed dark gray putty to the wheel's metal frame, down the cracks, and into the checkering. I work my way around the frame, trying to keep the PC-7 evenly distributed, in equal thickness. I haven't found it necessary to try to do the whole wheel at the same sitting. Since it takes so many stages to bring the wheel to its final splendor, at this point I'm pretty much just building the wheel up.

I want to warn you away from one error I made early on in my steering wheel artistry. I was worried about whether I was getting the epoxy all the way into the cracks and holes and not just smearing a thin veneer over the top. A lot of the damage was in the form of shallow, lens-shaped dents rather than deep holes and cracks, and I worried that any epoxy I was putting into these shallow holes might pop out as I proceeded through the rest of the sanding process.

So it occurred to me while I was working on another wheel at a different time, maybe if I drilled tiny holes into each of these lenses, cracks, and crevasses, I could then push the PC-7 well into the old rubber or new, setup wheel materials. Sort of like a dentist drills before he fills a tooth. Wrong-O.

I found that wherever I drilled a hole and pushed epoxy into it, a little worm of epoxy popped right back out. I have since learned that a very small slit is a much more reliable receptacle for the epoxy because it can be slid into the opening rather than pushed into a hole. Generally, however, PC-7 sticks pretty well to cured and solid PC-7. Good stuff.

I've tried a lot of different ways to get a really smooth surface on the PC-7, smoothing it down with an oily finger, a wet finger, more credit card pieces, a plain ol' Rogie finger. They all seem to work fine. I wondered if the water or oil might compromise the setting-up process of the epoxy, but no, it set up just fine. Ultimately the surface is going to depend on the further steps of filing, sanding, priming, and painting anyway.

Once I have the wheel pretty well covered with epoxy and the epoxy has cured to a thoroughly hard surface, I set up my workbench to file this first application down. I have never in all my experience been able to take an Allis-Chalmers steering wheel off its shaft. Never. Not even without regard for wrecking the wheel. So, I've just had to be content to work on the wheel with the shaft still attached.

I have set my work bench with a support downwind about 5 feet, on which I can rest the shaft while I'm working on the front or sides of the wheel and placed a hook on the ceiling where I can stick the shaft when I'm working on the back. I have a short length of 2x6 wood, across which I have tacked two shorter pieces of 2x2, so I can rest the wheel itself on the bench without danger of it rolling off and hitting the floor, shattering the old rubber or new epoxy. I pad the board with soft cloth or bits of old carpeting to protect the surface of the wheel.

First I take down the new epoxy roughly to the profile of the old rubber with 6-inch, fairly coarse files. I like the short, solid, multifaced files called "cobbler's rasps," but I also like to use half-round bastards, mostly because I like to tell people that I'm using half-round bastards. At this stage, the files aren't very fancy. You will want to have a convex file face for work on the inside of curves. A flat file will work fine for outside curves if you show a little care.

Files clog up frequently with epoxy, so you'll need a file brush to clean them just as frequently. I also blow mine out with compressed air, but you have to be very careful about blowing dust and debris around when you are working with new epoxy, primer, or paint. At this stage, however, it doesn't matter.

Then I go over the wheel again with finer files, coarse sandpaper, and rifflers (a kind of small, handled file that is convenient for funny curves in the wheel; you can find these in a good woodworking catalog). I have also used a utility knife to pare or shave off excess epoxy. A good knife cuts the epoxy easily; but I'm such a klutz, I prefer sanding or filing because it is much more conservative in removing excess, and I'm less likely to take off too much of the epoxy (or my finger) in my zeal to get the job done.

I really like the sponge sanders available in paint and hardware stores. They come in various grits, sometimes two on a single sponge. They are super for steering wheel work, where there is no such thing as a flat surface, and a lot of the curves are very tight and very complex. Some Allis and John Deere wheels have little finger indentations. Imagine sanding that with sandpaper on a wooden block!

After I get the wheel down pretty well (but not at all finished; we're not ready for that yet) I look it over very carefully. You will easily see where the irregularities are. They show up pretty well. Small, abrupt divots are even clearer because of the different appearance of the sanded to the untouched PC-7. At this point I am generally just hoping to have my repairs roughly in the same configuration as the original rubber. As you file and sand, watch carefully for how your repairs

> *Sex is good, but not as good as fresh sweet corn.*
> **—GARRISON KEILLOR**

match the old profile. Try to take off as much excess epoxy as you can without taking any of the original rubber off.

Now is also a good time to get ready to fill in remaining holes and divots by cutting (with a fine saw, knife, or file) slits and grooves over pits and dents. Then I blow off loose epoxy filings or dust. I try to make this happen about the time for a meal or evening break so when I come back there's not a lot of dust in the air. I also use a small shop vacuum to clean up around the shop desk to avoid fouling new work.

Next I mix up some more PC-7 and hope I've done a good enough job the first time around that I won't need a lot, but it doesn't often happen that way. I fill in all the low spots, holes, cuts, grooves, that kind of thing, put the wheel some place where it won't get bumped, and let it cure and set up. And then I go back to the filing and sanding, with ever finer files and grit.

When you are sanding, filing, or blowing off your work with a compressor nozzle, wear a mouth and nose mask to filter out the dust. I know it's inconvenient and looks funny (pretend like you're Jesse James, maybe that will make a mask easier to accept), but try one and then look at the outside of it. See all that junk stuck on the outside of the mask? Without the mask, that stuff would be in your lungs. No good. Disposable masks are cheap. They're probably not as good as a real, filtering shop mask, but even this little precaution can save you a lot of later discomfort, if not health problems.

There may be a need for even a third round of filling, filing, and sanding. That's okay. This is not craft; this is ART! After I had done three or four practice steering wheels, all good enough to go on a tractor, I took the ruined wheel off of Linda's still unrestored John Deere B and as a gift to her redid it. For that job, I even did a fourth filling, filing, and sanding. It is so pretty that when I finished it and took it to her in the sanctuary of her studio, I felt no embarrassment at all in putting it beside her finest paintings. That wheel now hangs like a Monet on the wall of my bedroom where I can see it and appreciate its beauty daily.

Don't rush the process. Don't get impatient. Those of you who have read my previous tractor treatises know that I strongly urge patience for the most knotty of problems, and I am not a guy naturally inclined toward patience. I just know it works. I can tell you from experience here that anything you don't take care of now is not going to heal itself. The slightest divot you leave in that wheel is going to be there when you are done, shining like my kindergarten painting *Sky and Earth* would at the Louvre, blaring painfully like my trumpet used to in the Lincoln High School band, where I held down the last chair in the trumpet section for three straight years, a record that has never been challenged in lo! these many years.

STEERING WHEELS:
THE OVERLOOKED MEDIUM

Once you have every hole, depression, scratch, and blemish filled and sanded, carefully tape off with masking tape the areas you don't want painted (that's why it's called "masking" tape), and apply a spray primer. I didn't do that on the first steering wheel I did, and that was a real mistake. Paint just kept soaking in. I suppose that wouldn't have been so bad if the same slightly roughened surface was all over the entire wheel. But the paint I applied next was shiny where there was old rubber and matte (dull) where I had filled in with epoxy. It took a lot of paint to cover that mistake.

After the primer dries (which is almost instantly, but I give it plenty of time to get hard because it sands more easily) I sand the wheel lightly again, leaving the masking tape on there. (By the way, when you use a spray can primer and paint like I do, when you finish with your job, turn the can upside down and spray for just a moment until just gas and no paint is coming out. Then you can store it without dry paint clogging up the nozzle.) Then I put on a second coat of primer. That may not be necessary, but ol' Rog, once he is twice burned, is triple wary.

I use Ace Hardware black matte, indoor/outdoor paint. I really like the stuff. It dries quickly and evenly and seems very resistant to running. Do follow the advice of keeping a good 12-inch distance between the nozzle and the wheel. That will cut down on running and give you a more even paint job.

I do my wheel-painting outside on a clear, warm, calm day. There aren't a lot of those in Nebraska, but generally, anything under a gale is considered calm here, and in the shelter of my shop's downwind side, I've never had any trouble. Be careful about what is downwind from you. I once hired a house painter who used one extra gallon of white paint turning my black Labs into dalmatians.

Here's where the inconvenience of those damn Allis-Chalmers unremovable steering shafts becomes an advantage: I rest the long, heavy shaft across my woodpile or a couple of sawhorses with small blocks of wood tacked about 2 feet apart on either side of the shaft. Then, as I paint, I can turn the wheel as well as move the spray can. This really gives me an even paint job and cuts back on running drips substantially.

Again, as was the case with the epoxy and primer, the spray paint dries quickly, but I always give it a good day to dry so it's very hard; easier to sand, harder to mar. I lightly sand the wheel and look it over to see how even my paint job is. At this point, it is not simply a matter of covering everything.

That's pretty easy to do because the primer is a much lighter color and you can see very clearly where you have missed. Now it's also a matter of getting an even job. I don't think you can do that with one coat. Besides, is this a job you want to get over and complete with the least cost and most net profit? If so, you're reading the wrong book and you're in the wrong hobby. Take your time. Do it right. Spray it again. If you are not absolutely happy with the results, do it again.

Remember, this is not a matter of pleasing others. I go through exactly this complicated process even with steering wheels I restore for fun and eventually store in the rafters of my shop's parts bay. Sure, I know that eventually when I kick off and Linda auctions all this stuff off, her new boyfriend will throw his arm over her shoulders, watch appreciatively as the bidding goes ever higher on that dang-near mint condition, factory-restored steering wheel, as crafted by the Old Master, Roger Welsch, Himself, and whisper in her ear, "Tinklebuns, you know, that Roger must have really been quite a guy." But I do it right anyway.

ART (NAKED WOMEN, THAT IS) IN THE SHOP

There is more art in my shop, of course, than steering wheels. The interior decorating in my shop is, uh, how shall I say it? Eclectic. I have lots of naughty-girl calendars because a guy can never know too well what day it is. In fact, I can also tell you what days of the week October 6, 1997, and April 25, 1998, fell on because those pages of my calendars did a particularly good job of calling my attention to the transitory nature of time, among other things.

I don't know how many times I have explained to Linda and daughter Antonia that even in the shop, I need to know what day it is. Oh, and whoops! You're right, that woman *is* nekkid as a jaybird! Linda has come to endure this appreciation I have for art photography. As she explains to disapproving visitors, "Sometimes it's just easier to keep an old engine idling than to have to jump-start it fresh every time."

On the other hand, I don't know how many times I have come out to my shop and found, with annoying frequency, that the calendar ladies have had little paper swimsuits pasted on them or that the art has been vandalized with comments like "She'd only kill you, Rog," or "Yeah, sure, Rog, dream on."

There has also been comment on the fact that certain favorite months have been detached from their calendars and saved on the wall until their calendral designations are history, and they themselves are so darkened by smoke, grease, dust, and dirt that they are more memory than mammary. On occasion I have torn off the days section of, for example, the particularly cheerful Ms. Tiffany of August so that the days of September appear beneath her and she graces my wall for an extra 30 days. Or six months, since Misses October, November, and December weren't all that perky.

I think this speaks well of me. It says I'm not fickle. I do not see these young and obviously friendly ladies as something to be torn off and casually thrown into the trash. No, I reward their loyalty with a loyalty of my own. As far as I'm concerned, Miss January from the Women of Texas 1999 Calendar will be on my shop wall as long as it is my shop wall because I can see she has a good heart, and I appreciate that.

Yeah, I know. Linda doesn't buy that either.

I don't have a lot of wall space to fill up with art because I use a system called "open storage." All tools or supplies I have are hanging on the wall. That way I can see them. When I am working on a tractor, I even hang parts (small ones in plastic bags) on wall pegs so I can keep track of them. Things I can't see are for all intents and purposes gone forever. They'll show up at my final sale too.

By way of other decorative arts, I have an aerial photo of Stromp's Dump, a local tractor salvage yard of considerable repute; a signed note paper from Dusty Hill, bass player and lead singer of ZZ Top; a signed poster and set of backstage tickets for a Beach Boys concert from Al Jardine, the very concert where Al invited me to come from backstage to sing "Good Vibrations" with them.

My walls sport a number of signs relevant to my interests ("Old Allis Retirement Home," "No Gurls," and the "Lava Lamp Philosophy," for example) and more selections of particularly healthy young ladies from the Women of Texas calendar of a couple of years ago. Oh, wait a minute. I already told you about the calendars. Funny how an old man's mind can drift. . . .

A few years ago I resolved to stop some of the winter heat loss from my shop doors by sticking large sheets of foam plastic insulation to them, and I have used old license plates to do that since without the plates, sheet rock screws will pull right on through. (By the way, you really want to be careful while turning those spray paint cans upside down and emptying the excess paint before storing. I once did that up against the insulation foam and it melted like ice cream under a welding torch.)

I have a couple of posters and banners I've picked up. A NASCAR banner from Eric's Tavern, a Jimi Hendrix poster Linda gave me for Christmas, some drawings Antonia did of my tractors and me many years ago, and a picture of a glass of port wine and a plate of Stilton cheese, crackers, some

English walnuts, and a sliced pear, the single most delicious food combination in the world.

The real art of my shop, however, is the tools on the wall and hanging from the ceiling rafters. When I go into the Craftsman area of our local Sears store, I enter it with the kind of reverence usually reserved for art galleries. Look at those things; shiny and solid, flowing lines, clean and clear, an unmistakable message. To tell you the truth, I don't know, if the choice were to paint a picture of a naked woman or a professional quality 1 1/4-inch Craftsman combination wrench, or (gasp!) a Snap-On, well, I don't know a lot about art, but I do know what I like.

THE SOUND OF MUSIC

But there is more to the fine arts than canvas and marble, naked girls and rock posters.

What of music? I find myself relenting in my dotage about this category. I am an unabashed, hopeless, card-carrying, overaged hippie. No sense in denying it. In my shop (and for that matter, for maybe a quarter-mile in every and any direction) the music is ZZ Top, the Rolling Stones, Jethro Tull, Crosby, Stills, Nash, and Young, The Incredible String Band, Queen, The Band, Lynyrd Skynyrd, Cream, Janis Joplin, Jimi Hendrix, and Creedence Clearwater Revival, not necessarily in that order, but necessarily at full volume.

You may find this hard to believe, but Linda will not, that I have actually blown out large, industrial-grade speakers while playing these Old Masters on my 25x25-foot shop stereo. (Oh, I forgot to mention, a lot of the blood I refer to in the chapter about shop first-aid problems was from my ears. Right up there with safety goggles, face shields, and welding gloves, I recommend ear mufflers or plugs. Mostly for my neighbors a quarter-mile away. I don't want to miss one subtlety of ZZ Top's "Nationwide," thank you.)

But I'm not stuffy about this. One of my favorite quotes in the world is Bob Newhart's incredibly precise observation, "I don't like country music, but I don't mean to denigrate those who do. And for the people who like country music, denigrate means 'put down.'" I know this isn't going to make me a lot of friends, but country and western music makes my skin crawl. Those phony damn whiners and moaners. But no, let's be kind here, and let's consider self-preservation: Linda adores C-W music. If it wasn't for her, I'd be willing to fistfight anyone who mistakes that howling for music.

She explained this to me, and upon reflection, I think she's right: Music serves different purposes. Linda says country and western music calms her. Sure, it all sounds the same and is dreary, self-serving complaining, but those are the lyrics. She doesn't hear the words; what she hears are consistent, calm, quiet, predictable rhythms and patterns. What she needs are consistent, calm, quiet, predictable rhythms and patterns. She wants to have long, slow moments in which to contemplate color, value, composition, and to think through the process.

Of course that doesn't work for me! I want exhilaration. I want 10 more cups of coffee. I want to be able to rebuild an engine in six minutes. I want to scrub the living hell out of a filthy piston so that it's gleaming-new right now! I want to dance (but only in my shop). I want to be recharged, energized, powered, jolted into action.

So I suggest that in your shop, when it comes to music, you consider what it is you want and need. My Old Man never listened to anything but polkas in his shop. (I guess his metabolic needs were braunschweiger and strudel.) I can imagine someone restoring old tractors to the sounds of Beethoven's symphonies (especially the Ninth). Sinatra? Sure. The Backstreet Boys? Of course. Rap? Well, uh . . .

Most of all, I can imagine someone working in a shop to no music at all. I can very easily imagine a mechanic wanting nothing more but the hum of a compressor, the snore of a good black Lab, maybe the gurgle of a parts cleaner, and the sound of the wind against the windows. But don't let the sound in your shop be an accident. It is as important to your final product, soul-restoration, as your tools and supplies.

If you are anything like me, and God help you if you are, you spend more time in your shop than you do at your dinner table. Or with your wife, as she is almost certain to have mentioned to you now and then somewhere along the line. So, doesn't it just make sense to spend some time making your shop a comfortable place to play, uh, work?

I believe from the bottom of my heart that a really good sound system is crucial to a good shop; I prefer a CD changer with as many slots as possible so I can play those ZZ Top classics without having to handle the CDs. They are easier to keep clean than old LP discs or tapes, but nonetheless it's really nice just to be able to punch a filthy, greasy finger at a button than try to gently pick up a disc and insert it into a slot.

I used to have a radio, but lightning blew it out about three times a year and the insurance company thinks that no one really needs a radio in the shop. I used the radio primarily to keep me alert and awake when working on a particularly boring or dangerous activity. My trick is to turn on Dr. Laura Schlessinger, that miserable, autocratic, arrogant, insufferable, intolerant, ignorant, humorless, hypocritical slut. I listen to her tell women how they should immediately dump any guy who has a naughty-girl calendar in his shop, knowing all the while that some of us have seen (and admittedly enjoyed) the porno shots she posed for to tweak her boyfriend's libido— not all that long ago. The only drawback for this is that I come into the house at the end of the day still growling and with a sore throat from screaming at the radio speaker.

I also have a TV, but I rarely turn it on. I like to work in my shop during the Indy 500. About the best place to watch the Indy 500 other than Indianapolis, is in fact, in a shop, according to a recent, nationwide poll. I think I heard that some place.

I know what you're thinking. You're thinking, "Wait a minute! Rog is a writer. So where is the section on 'Your Shop and the Language Arts'?!" Well, you big dummy, I've saved the best for last, just the same as I eat cake—the doughy crap first and THEN the frosting. Actually, this book and most of my others are a tribute to the glories of first-class story-telling. I love it when Woodrow, Lunchbox, Bunkie, Melvin Nelson, Mel Halsey, or Boswell Flick drop by the shop. Generally, I despise and avoid droppers-in. There's nothing more annoying than someone interrupting a man's spiritual meditations. It is essentially a matter of saying, "Screw your schedule. I have some free time, and here I am, so pay attention to me."

Not when these tractor buddies drop into the shop. When these guys come by, one of several things might happen, or several of several things. They may look over whatever I'm working on and decide, well, why not get this done? And do it. Or they may just feel I'm in need of a break. Or they may be dropping something off; jerky, a dead raccoon for the Coyotes in the bottom ground, some firewood they found somewhere, some extra safety awards they received at work. Or they may just sit down and want to tell stories, and my priorities are indeed good stories before tractor play, uh, work. Or they may do all those things.

Whatever they have in mind, it is almost never a matter of using up my time, as is the case with most droppers-in. These guys, real pals, are delivering, not picking up, and they generally deliver oral literature. After all, it was Lunchbox who taught me one of the most important and useful pieces of poetry I have ever heard in any shop, yet memorized: "Righty tighty, lefty loosey."

TALKIN' THE TALK

I am not a trained or even an experienced mechanic. I don't know how a lot of things are done. I don't know much about a lot of tools. I don't know about a lot of techniques. Most of all, I don't know a lot of the proper language. And just as there is a language of poetry, music, sculpture, wine, calendar photography, black Labs, and other of the arts, there is a distinct language of the antique tractor mechanic.

Car engines freeze up; tractor motors get stuck. You pound on a tent stake or stuck pickup tailgate; you beat on a stuck motor. "Mag" = magneto, and "carb" = carburator (always, by the way, spelled that way by mechanics, despite what your dictionery [sic] tries to tell you). There is a wonderful language of parts and tools: cylinder hones, pullers, valve spring compressors, angle grinders, stick welders. My major in college was modern languages; French and German have nothing on the language of the mechanic's shop.

One dimension of old tractor talk I'm nowhere close to mastering is the designation of tractors by model numbers and letters. My eyes glaze over when guys around me start talking tractors. You've been there. You know what I'm talking about:

FERD: My pappy never drove nothin' but a B 10, and I don't blame him. Ain't never been no tractor could match a B 10 in that sticky bottom ground we had.

RUF: Well, then you obviously never sat on the seat of a DM 114. Why, with that big square bottom 630 motor in it and the after-purchase DCD trannie, there wadn't no way a B 10 would outpull a DM 114.

CLARENCE: But for fun, you gotta have yer DD3. You coodn't chain and pull a wet cigar butt with a DD3 without turning the thing over backward on the drawbar, especially them Grade 3 JD drawbars. You know, the ones with the 770 pins at the end.

FERD, RUF, CLARENCE: Yup, yup, yup. Hey, Eric! We need another round over here. Make mine another MD 20/20.

> *Isn't that just about the prettiest thing you've ever seen?*
> **—DICK DAY, TURNING HIS BACK TO THE GLORIOUS AND GORGEOUS SASHA AND FIXING HIS GAZE INSTEAD ON A BATTERED, RUSTY JOHN DEERE B TRACTOR**

Moreover, there is something particularly baffling about the fact that none of the tractor numbers and letters mean a thing. I've asked the experts. I've asked owners and collectors and manufacturers and historians. So far as I can tell, an Oliver 99 was named a 99 because it was bigger than an 88, and therefore the 88 was bigger than an 80. The tractor was called an 80 because, well, someone in the office, maybe the lady who filled out time cards, was born in 1880. Or wanted an 80-cent raise. Or needed to lose 80 pounds.

When I started off on this tractor stuff, I had an Allis-Chalmers WC and since I didn't know diddly-squat about tractors, I presumed that the letters *W* and *C* stood for something. I spent cold, snowy evenings in front of my woodstove thinking about that. Maybe the designer was Walter Chesterton or something like that. Maybe the factory where this particular model was built was in West Carter, Wisconsin. Maybe the letters referred to a technical feature of the machine like "Wankel Cylinders," or "wobble-free calibration," or "won't choke."

But no, apparently the letters were just plucked from the air by someone who thought it would be a good idea to have this model designated by two letters, maybe one from toward the back of the alphabet and, uh, therefore, the next somewhat closer to the front.

It was only natural, therefore, that the next model be designated the Allis-Chalmers WD. (What did you expect, you big silly?) And the next after that, C. And B. And WD—aw, what the hell—40. In most cases language is a system; tractor language is a whim in a chaos in a shambles.

HAUTE CUISINE

In another book, *Diggin' In and Piggin' Out*, I treated American, and especially American male culinary arts, in the general sense of the world around us. I didn't deal with shop food there because shop food is a very special and specialized topic. All of this is to emphasize that I take food and the study of food seriously. I have given some considerable thought to this art form.

For example, you may know me as the inventor and distributor of Roger Welsch's Extra Fancy Combination Stink Bait and Sandwich Spread. And let this underscore another of my virtues: I'm not the sort just to see a problem and complain about it. No, I see a problem and I set about doing something to solve it!

I noticed from my first experiences with dough balls, chicken guts, stink bait, and blood clots (you know, the sort of things catfish really love, or fishermen think they really love) that they do not go well together with, say, braunschweiger and onion sandwiches. Let us put aside for the moment the very real and tragic likelihood that fouling stink bait lures with braunschweiger and onions would almost certainly distract mightily from the effectiveness of anyone's fishing success. Another coincidental consequence is that your braunschweiger and onion sandwich is going to taste like stink bait. In fact, so will the gingersnaps, brownies, oranges, lutefisk, anchovies, Limburger canapés, and just about anything and everything else you are intending to eat while you drag in the lunkers.

To my mind, it's a miracle no one else has ever struck on my solution, Roger Welsch's Extra Fancy Combination Stink Bait and Sandwich Spread, but no one did. I imagine the same could be said about the theory of relativity. It's not that Einstein invented the theory. He discovered it. It was there all along, but no one else had the massive brainpower it took to see it. Same with my combination stink bait and sandwich spread. I refuse to take credit for inventing the brilliant idea. It was there all along and I discovered it.

A lot of people have told me, by the way, that my combo stink bait and sandwich spread is just about as good as dynamite. Okay, so they're referring to its application as sandwich spread rather than bait. Nonetheless . . . (This fine product can be obtained, I might note, from the Gifte Shoppe of the National Liars Hall of Fame, 197th and Y Streets, Loading Dock M; Mail Drop 104; Attn: Marie, Dannebrog NE 68831-9759.)

I am now working on a shop equivalent. If you have ever grabbed a quick peanut butter and jelly sandwich, some potato chips, and a root beer out in your shop while in the middle of changing tractor transmissions, you have probably noticed the uncanny inevitability of the sandwich tasting like clutch dust, the potato chips tasting like Liquid Wrench, and the root beer taking on the distinct tang of parts cleaner.

Our research-and-development people are working at this very minute in the National Liars Hall of Fame labs to come up with an answer to the problem, but for the nonce, let me suggest the following: Ask your wife or significant other to come out to the shop at noon with a tray of goodies, which she can then delicately drop into your mouth, perhaps even as you continue your work on the transmission. I know what you are thinking, and maybe even saying, "Look, you idiot, if I were to ask my wife to drop black olives into my mouth while I lay on a creeper in the shop under a tractor, she'd [fill in appropriate violent action] my [fill in relevant body part] with a [choose one: sharp, hot, big, hard, cold, industrial, dull, Bavarian] [fill in tool designation]."

I've covered that problem too: Go to your local college's arts, sciences, or humanities offices and ask if you couldn't perhaps help some young student work her way through college by serving as your shop assistant. Tell her not to wear anything she doesn't want to get dirty. In fact, make it an even more attractive job by offering to provide shop clothing; an old loose shirt of yours, maybe overalls, anything at all. We're just talking shop clothes here, after all, and since it's going to be hot in the shop anyway, she probably shouldn't wear too much. (Don't ask dumb questions; it's going to be hot in the shop even if she goes on the job in mid-February.)

It's dirty, hot work and sometimes even close. Two people, one differential—not a lot of room there around that rear end, if you catch my drift. So don't be stingy when it comes to what could be a genuinely charitable act of paying a starting wage of, say, oh, $22 an hour. Don't worry about needing extra tools and equipment just because you now have a helper. How many creepers can a guy afford to buy? Plenty of room for two on that deluxe model the Little Lady got you last year for Christmas, right? There will be long hours. Nothing more fun than working late at night out in the shop with the snow falling gently against the window, the glow of the wood stove, the soft sounds of ZZ Top coming from the sound system . . .

My bet is that it won't be another noon go by before the Queen of the House is out there stuffing food into your mouth without a complaint until she can order and get delivery on three cases of Roger Welsch's Extra Fancy Combination Grease Buster, Bearing Lube, and High Protein Chip Dip. Patent Pending.

I don't have a coffeepot out in the shop, and I'm not going to until I can work a deal with the Liquid Wrench people to come up with an extra fancy combination thread penetrant/coffee formula.

Actually and seriously, I even learned not to keep much in the way of drink in my shop at all, or to take any out there. Long ago I was working with some friends at rebuilding an ancient log house for a museum. Evening had come and we were working on supper, getting ready for the evening, cleaning up, all that end-of-the-day kind of thing. I had a quart bottle of Old Milwaukee in one hand by way of a preprandial quaff, and I had an Old Mil quart bottle full of kerosene in my other hand, with which I was filling lanterns. I got to talking about something and lost my focus. (I know. Hard to imagine.) I ranted about something, took a drink of beer, filled one lantern, ranted about something else, filled another lantern, took a drink of kerosene.

YIKES! I drank kerosene! Actually, it wasn't all that bad. Maybe it was just not so bad in comparison with Old Milwaukee. Hard to say. I know my Old Man said they used to get a dose of kerosene and sulfur every spring for "spring complaint," so I wasn't worried about dying, but still, it's not what I expected. I spouted kerosene over everyone in front of me, including a young beauty who made a pass at me later that evening. So I'm not really saying drinking kerosene is a bad thing, exactly.

What I am saying is that in my shop today, lo! these many years later, I don't want to drink a lot of the stuff I have sitting around. And drinking Southern Comfort or single malt Scotch only encourages this kind of error, I find. So I don't do much by way of bartending in my shop. Sometimes I take a bottle of mineral water out there, perhaps to flush out the taste of something I have nonetheless swigged by mistake, but that's about it. I don't like to take a cup of coffee out there because I almost inevitably forget instantaneously where I set the cup. That's not the real problem, though; the real problem is that a few weeks later I find the cup again and have to explain to Linda why her favorite "Jamaica Swings" cup now has a fantasy garden of green and black stuff growing in it.

Why, you ask, don't I just keep a small fridge with cold beer? Can't hardly mistake a bottle of Engine Honey for a can of beer, after all! If a can of beer is ruined when you spill Mystic Oil in it, well, you can just throw it away with no real loss—at least not the loss of a wee tout of squandered Aberlour single malt Scotch whisky. If you lose a beer in the shop, well jeez, you expect to lose the occasional can of beer in a shop!

Besides, aluminum beer cans are super for cutting bearing shims, at least for an Allis WC. Did you know the middle of a beer can is thinner than the sides toward the top or bottom of the can? It is. That means, you can not only cut shims from a beer can, you can also get varying thicknesses of a very delicate kind so you can get exact clearances on the bearing caps and torques on the bolts holding them. Wow. It's almost worth having a few cold brews sitting around just for parts.

There is a problem: Cold beer attracts pests. In my case, that's usually Woodrow, Bunkie, and Lunchbox. You know, guys like that. So, when I need some help with a stuck piston, mistimed mag, baffling carb, or utterly indecipherable shop manual, I go up to Eric's Tavern and ask Eric what it is those guys drink. I know they drink Old Mil Lite, but I am not only buying beer here, I am sending out the message. I buy a case of cold Old Mil Lite. It won't be two hours before the word gets out about my purchase up at Eric's and those guys are sitting around my shop, drinking that case of beer, and working on my problem.

On the other hand, when I want a long, quiet afternoon or evening in my shop, enjoying the solitude and peace of my own thoughts, I don't buy a case of cold Old Mil.

CHAPTER 10

WOMEN

A man's friend likes him but leaves him as he is; his wife
loves him and is always trying to turn him into something else.
—**G. K. CHESTERTON**

C
an't live with 'em, can't live with 'em. As they say around here. Or ought to. So, why have I left the chapter devoted to my discussion of the feral sex until so late in the book? Because I'm scared as a rabbit, that's why. Here I am, about to spill everything we guys talk about in duck blinds, on THTs, in shops on winter days, or maybe when window-peeking over at the new school marm's house. I mean, the only females who have ever been let in on this stuff up to now are golden retrievers named Goldie. It is not at all my intent to let this lit dynamite go public, and that's why this book is not available for sale to women. But we need to get this out to young men as soon as possible, and then we've got to start sticking together.

I've known this for a long time. I didn't buy Linda a wedding ring until we'd been married 10 years because it just didn't make sense to me to make that kind of commitment before I was absolutely certain where things stood. Not that I now know where things stand, you understand. I just finally got tired of waiting for everything to fall into place. As did Linda.

Nor is this a matter of me suggesting that we men do something women didn't do long, long, long ago. You've heard the little hints and suggestions I've made; that there is a Woman School, and they do learn things there, and that they do work as a single, unified, male-crushing machine. I once came home from town all downhearted because I found out a good ol' buddy of mine was about to get married again, late in life. His first wife had died, and obviously he'd been lonely for a couple years, but still, I was concerned. I told Linda I sure hoped Marv wasn't going to get married and have this new woman in his life squeeze the life, joy, and spirit out of him.

That's what happened only a year before to our friend Duane, who also lost his wife, took up with another lady late in life and was reduced to going to Tupperware parties and church bake sales for entertainment. Linda looked at me quizzically and asked, "Why should he be any different from the rest of you?"

I don't know what that means to you, but to me it means there is a unified plot on the part of women of all ages to reduce us free-spirited, big-picture philosophers (which is to say, men) to gray blobs of quivering protoplasm, each and every one of us.

Which is not to say that women get along hunky-dory with each other regularly. Only under certain circumstances do they join forces. I think we, you and I, know what those circumstances are. I happen to know that this too is a matter of biology, not accident or culture. By way of evidence I offer the following anecdote:

I was once at an operation where hundreds of wild horses, fresh off the open range, were being sorted for sale and distribution. We had unloaded the stallions and now had a truck full of mares to deal with. "I imagine the mares will be a lot easier to handle, right?" I asked the wrangler in charge, me knowing about as much about horses as I (or any other men) know about women.

The old horseman who was honchoing the work chuckled and said, "A lot of folks ask that, but that's not the way it goes. Look over there. See? The stallions are standing there on that hill, shivering and confused, wondering just what the hell is going to happen to them next. They're too busy with the situation to worry about each other; but when these mares come down the chutes, they will proceed to kick the living hell out of each other, especially if they have colts, and they'll do that until we get rid of them sometime next week.

"When I'm in the operations shack and I hear all hell breaking loose out here with the mustangs, I don't have to guess where to look. It won't be the stallions. No, they're still just standing there. It'll be in the corral with the mares. They just cannot get along together for more than a few minutes at a time without getting into a hellacious fight—kicking, biting, bucking, screaming, knocking each other around."

He paused for dramatic effect. ". . . Unless some poor stupid damned stud manages to get through the fence separating the two pens. And at that point, all the mares will turn their attention on him and proceed to pound him down into about 2 pounds of hair and teeth. It's as if they blame him for getting them into this fix. Ain't that something?"

Well, yes, that is something, because I've had the same feeling all too often myself, having no idea where I was, how I got there, or why all those women seemed so angry at me all the time.

Who invented chess? Anyone around here know? Of course you don't. Chess is an incredibly complex game devised thousands of years ago and polished to its present diamond-like finish by thousands of generations of the best thinkers in the world, of both genders, of all nations and religions, of all layers, permutations, castes, and philosophies of mankind. Chess is, in short, about as close as you can get to a distillation of the human condition.

If you don't know anything about chess, well, for what I'm about to observe you don't need to know much. Ask someone who knows anything at all about chess how some of the pieces move. It's not like checkers; the pieces in chess move in different patterns around the board. The bishop in the obtuse lines of religion, the rook or castle in the straight lines of military architecture, the pawns (simple soldiers) move straight ahead to almost inevitable destruction. Now, what about the queen and king?

The king is most important, right? The game is over when the king is slain. The words *check mate*, in fact, come from the old words *shah maht*, meaning "The king is dead." How does the king, this most important of board characters, move? One step in any direction. Well, that's pretty appropriate. No other piece on the board can move in so many directions.

Except one. The queen. The queen moves in any direction too, any number of squares. The queen is without question the most powerful piece on the board. It is quite expected that the deathblow will be dealt the king by the queen. It is virtually impossible for the king to kill the queen. Does that age-old metaphor say anything to you?

I used to be a beekeeper until I discovered that bees hate me and love nothing more than to inflict pain on me. I think it's because I know too much about bees. Do you know how a beehive works? The bee colony consists of three kinds of bees. Most of the bees in a hive are females, there are a few males around, and there is the queen, who runs everything. Only females have stingers. Only females run things.

A new queen looks around at the choice of males in the hive, chooses one, goes on a nuptial flight with the Chosen One, has sex with him (lucky guy) and then on the way back to the hive, having taken his reproductive juices, kills him. Yep, you read that right. One guy gets lucky, sort of, and the object of his affections then kills him.

The women keep a few male bees around, just in case something happens to the queen and they need another one. The original queen uses the same contribution from that first male the rest of her life, not ever needing to top off, so to speak. The females can make more or fewer males as they need. And when fall comes and supplies get a little short, well, who needs males around? So the ladies of the happy village just kill all the males and kick the corpses off the front porch into the leaves on the ground below. If they need a male or two in the spring, well, what the hell, they'll just make a couple of new ones.

No, dear, I am not saying anything at all about what that may or may not mean. I just thought it would be interesting reading for my tractor-lovin' buddies.

I realize I'm walking on thin ice here. What happens if this does fall into the wrong hands and gets passed around at Woman School? Well, that's like asking what happens if Saddam Hussein gets 854 billfold-size atomic bombs. It sure won't be good, and it especially won't be good for us men.

I am still baffled by the number of letters I got after *Old Tractors and the Men Who Love Them* and *Busted Tractors and Rusty Knuckles* were published from guys who wanted me to get them out of the fix they had gotten themselves into by—get this— reading the books at night in bed. Talk about stupid! They'd get to laughing and their wives or significant others would get interested and want to know what the book was about, and the dummies would read out loud whatever part of the book they were reading! Jeez.

Worse yet, some men wrote me that they woke their wives up (and why would anyone do that?!) to read them something from the book. Usually a passage when I was talking about stuff men do in their shops or making fun of what women do not do in men's shops. These guys obviously have never read anything about bees.

I also got letters from women. I don't even want to talk about them. Ugly stuff. (And what exactly is a Manchurian Soprano Maker anyway?)

So, read this book someplace in the open where you can see women coming from a couple of hundred yards off. Carry a little bottle of steak sauce with you, and when you discover a woman approaching, pour sauce on the book and eat the sucker just as fast as you can.

As an alternative, glue a permanent page marker on this page so you can find it immediately and open right to it. Stay calm. Open the book to this page. As she gets within earshot, start reading the following passage slowly and intently, nodding your head as you do. If she asks what you're reading, say, "Oh, nothing." If she insists, tell her you're embarrassed because it's a book on the Sensitive Man and what he can do to make the woman in his life happy. Very happy.

If her probing continues, read the following:

❊ ❊ ❊ ❊ ❊

It is important to remember any and all important anniversaries of your relationship, your wife's birthday, St. Valentine's Day, Christmas, and anything else whatsoever she might consider worth remembering. Dates like this shouldn't be hard to remember, especially if you forget them once. Buy her something nice: chocolates, flowers, expensive jewelry, a gift certificate to someplace other than Victoria's Secret, or a new automobile. [Nod your head, stupid, as if you understand what you are reading and agree enthusiastically with it.] But don't make affection and generosity a function solely of important days. Make every day an important day. Read poetry to her; better yet, memorize it and whisper it to her at sometime other than when she's vacuuming the carpet. Buy pretty, sentimental cards for all occasions (it is no longer acceptable to buy one expensive one at the beginning of your relationship and initial it every year afterward), but now and then just buy one because, well, gosh, she's in your heart. [Look lovingly at her, smile, and nod again. Quick.]

Let's all remember, my male friends, we are talking here about the Light of Our Lives.

✳ ✳ ✳ ✳ ✳

If that hasn't worked so far, it's not going to work.

Recite the Male Generic Apology now. It's outlined on page 181. Better yet, have it tattooed on your forehead and just blink your eyes.

Okay, now, let's get down to business. Man, what's going on with women anyway? I simply cannot get out of my mind the chorus of the old Irish folksong, "Ah, the devil's in the women, and they never can go easy." Isn't that really about all we guys want, just a little easy goin', right?

As I was telling you before about how to handle any discovery that you are indeed reading this book, and finding out just about everything you need to know about women, I

mentioned the recurring problem men have remembering
all the dates we are required to remember. It's not that
they're so scattered throughout the year or that they're not
important, in my mind at least.

There is, in my situation, Christmas in late December, followed fairly quickly by St. Valentine's Day in February. Then in
March there is Linda's birthday. In April is our anniversary, and
May, of course, hosts Mother's Day. In June there is the anniversary of the first time she came to my bachelor pad and used the
bathroom, in which I had forgotten to put toilet paper. A lapse
that is also remembered annually. (My son-in-law Andrew's
wedding toast comes to mind: "On this day I am forgetting all my
past loves, mistakes, sins, lapses, and failures. No point in both
Joyce and I remembering the same things, after all.") July is, oh,
something, and August is a Czech Bohemian festival of some sort
where the husband has to buy his wife a gift, and September . . .

Well, you get the idea. But, know what? I consider myself
a lucky man. Linda figured out fairly early in our relationship (I think it was the first time she came to my bachelor pad
and discovered there was no toilet paper in the bathroom)
that I am not a detail man. Me, I work with the Big Picture
and leave the details for others to mop up. Almost 20 years
ago now (I think it was on St. Valentine's Day) Linda showed
up with a frilly, mushy card that set us back about six bucks
and a big heart-shaped box of candy. She said that this way
she could pretty well figure she was going to get something for
Valentine's Day, whatever else happened. Or didn't happen.
She had me sign the card and she put it on the counter in the
kitchen, where it would remind her of what a sensitive lug I
can be when the occasion demands.

She did the same for all ensuing gift-requisite days
throughout that year, and what a blessed relief that was, for

both of us. Here's the best thing about the arrangement: She saved all the cards and boxes and brings them out every year on the appropriate days. I initial them, stamp them with the date, sometimes write in encouraging and romantical comments like "Good year, Hon. Keep up the good work," or "You could use a little improvement in the area of sympathy for a guy with a bad cold but other than that, you've done well enough this year to rate a 'superior' ranking," that kind of thing. Yes, the first year of this investment was something of a setback for the family budget, but if you amortize the payout over a few years, well, it really starts to look like a pretty fair expenditure.

A mixed marriage leads inevitably to discomfort and conflict, and yet men persist in marrying women.
—GEORGE SCHWELLE

Damn sight cheaper than a divorce, I can tell you.

Women, on the other hand, blithely forget any of our important days of the year; the anniversary of when Sweet Allis came to live with us, the dogs' birthdays, the day you won the hearts of your buddies up at the tavern by sucking 37 eggs, that kind of thing.

No, not all women are as reasonable as Linda is with her cards and heart-shaped boxes. Not even all reasonable women are that reasonable. The following is a fairly accurate dialogue transcribed from not only the last road trip I took with Woodrow and Lunchbox, but every road trip I've ever taken with Woodrow and Lunchbox.

ME: Well, this is a pretty good start, actually. You dumb @#$%s are only a little over an hour late. I thought we said seven in the morning.

WOODROW: Same old story. I got to that idiot Lunchbox's house, and he wasn't even out of bed yet. You'd think a guy who's been married more than five years would be tired of that by now.

LUNCHBOX: Well, you know the likelihood of me being late because of that, I . . . ooops. Excuse me . . .

ME AND WOODROW: My God, man, what did you eat last night? That's the most disgusting thing I've ever smelled in my life. Jeez, that's rotten! You're disgusting. I'd rather ride in back with the hogs than you. Lunchbox, you're a pig.

LUNCHBOX: Yeah, it probably wasn't a good idea to eat onion soup and bean burritos the night before a road trip, but I figured you miserable dogs would be right at home with the smell. Speaking of which, Welsch, what the hell did you roll in that makes you smell so bad?

ME: Well, actually, these are the same clothes I wore to go fishing down at the creek yesterday. New stink bait I'm trying.

WOODROW: Man, that stuff sure is rotten. I hope the fish like it. Wow. Does this window open, Lunchbox?

LUNCHBOX: Just swing the door open a while. Between that and the holes in the floor she'll air out real quick. Here, have some breakfast.

ME: Hey, how long have these Cheetos been under your front seat? The expiration date says "Eat Before End of Civil War," and this venison jerky is more hair than meat. Perfect. Just the way I like it. Breakfast of champions . . .

WOODROW: Lunchbox, you half-wit, this beer is warm. It's 10 degrees below freezing. How do you get warm beer when it's cold out?

LUNCHBOX: Actually, I came out this morning and it was frozen because I left it in the truck all night. So I put it on the engine block on the way over here to thaw it out. Watch out when you open that.

ME: AW JEEZ, LUNCHBOX, YOU DAMN #$%@%. BEER
EVERYWHERE. I'M SOAKED!

WOODROW: Well, one thing for sure: You sure do smell better now that you've had a shower.

You get the idea. Men not only don't mind being told
they smell bad, they'd just as soon not do a lot of traveling
with some guy who tells them they smell good.

For the moment, compare that with the following excerpt
from a conversation I had yesterday with Linda and Antonia,
and will almost certainly have with them again today:

ME: Good morning, Snookums. Hi, Darling. Glorious day out
there. You both look very nice. Coffee sure smells good.

ANTONIA: I knew this sweater was all wrong with these shoes,
but you didn't have to throw it in my face!

ME: Uh, but uh, you look just fine. I just said . . .

ANTONIA: If you let me buy more than one miserable pair of
shoes a week, I wouldn't have this problem! [Runs up
stairs sobbing]

LINDA: I do my best with the coffee. You never like my coffee
no matter what I do.

ME: I like your coffee. I . . .

LINDA: I don't care how your mother made coffee. This is
how I make coffee. And why are you always so grumpy in
the morning anyway? [Runs up stairs sobbing]

ME, to dogs: Hi, Thud! Hi, Lucky! How are my good boys?
Oh, you're absolutely stunning this morning. And whatever you rolled in sure does stink! [Dogs wag tails. Rog
wags tail and heads for shop.]

For years I have wondered about the whole thing with
smell. Men tend to laugh at really bad odors. Women don't.

Men think really bad smells are hilarious. I've been camping with both men and women. Men can go interminable lengths of time without bathing or without being offended that no one else is bathing. Women can't. At least that's what I thought, but I didn't want to say much about my opinion because I might be labeled a pervert or idiot or both. Not that I've never been labeled a pervert or idiot or both, but I just didn't want to provide any more grist for that particular mill.

A couple of weeks ago, however, I saw a show on the A&E channel entitled "Love Chronicles." It was fascinating. It had some things to say about love, sex, marriage, and romance (nothing about tractors, unfortunately and inevitably) that I particularly enjoyed because they reinforced precisely what I've believed for decades.

And there were a few surprises too. Get this: They said research has shown that women like the smell of pumpkin pie, lilacs, and pastry. They do not like the smell of braised meat. Foofoo water does not move them. Nor does it impress a man. In fact, the scientists have found that nothing seems to impress a man by way of the smell or taste of a woman; he simply doesn't care. But (God, I love this one), men DO like the taste and smell of alcohol on a woman. Well, duh.

And yet, in the very moment I write this, my e-mail signal boings and I find a note from a friend with whom I shared the above paragraph. He writes,

"In my younger days the smell of alcohol on a woman turned up my thermostat considerably, and I'm not kidding. Of course, those were the days when the need to breed and replicate was considerably stronger. On the surface, I believe the smell of alcohol might trigger the 'she's easy' response in men. But I also believe, even more strongly, that this particular smell also triggers a deep, subliminal 'she's willing' response in men. 'Hey, look, I'm drinking, and I want to have fun and, say, is that a gun in your pocket?'

"Which is more evil or socially acceptable? At those times I didn't care. 'Breed, breed, breed' was echoing in my Cro-Magnon mind.

"Signed: Studmuffin"

I would argue with my friend about him being a Cro-Magnon. They were a fairly advanced people. Mostly I resent him complicating the issue with his oh-so-civilized, oh-so-fine line between "easy" and "fun." No one loves an impossibility, do they? I mean, I don't know. I'm asking here.

The Trouble with marriage is that while every woman is at heart a mother, every man is at heart a bachelor.

Women are therefore almost completely wrong in their assessments of how a man's taste and smell buds work. Men have a much better grasp on how a woman works, at least in this very restricted physiological arena. Okay, sometimes I forget, but I do know there are consequences to inattention to olfactory issues. I remember with some trepidation Linda's pan-review of *The Britches of Madison County*. "Well, sure," she sniffed. "Any woman would be thrilled by the prospect of a man drifting through and leaving again just about the time he needs to have his laundry done."

The point being, the guy had the sense to move on too, he being no dummy. This is the male sensitivity I was talking about. Perhaps the most vivid example my research has uncovered of this male awareness of the sensitivity of the feminine sniffer was a time when I was on a commercial canoe trip. A group of about 20 families was taking the float down Nebraska's beautiful Niobrara River; I was along as campfire entertainment, which I used to do quite often.

I got to know the grunts on these trips pretty well. Everyone had a lot of jobs: cooking, hauling, setting up camps, dragging canoes off of rocks and snags, cutting firewood, hauling water, and so on. It was tough work, but it was also a wonderful environment in which to work.

Well, on this trip a friend of mine, a grunt named Phil Pfeiffer, a name I will use because his real name is, well, uh, Phil Pfeiffer, fell immediately and hopelessly in love with Tami, lovely daughter of one of our clients. I mean immediately, and I mean hopelessly. We were two hours into this trip, and he was already damn near killing himself to impress this woman. It was obvious (and hilarious) to all of us what was going on. And a little, well, gosh, heartwarming. You know, young love and all.

So we reach the end of the trip and the bus with the clients takes off to a little town where we would all gather for a big celebratory supper to finish off the trip. The rest of us loaded canoes, cleaned and packed equipment, washed up dishes and cooking gear, hauled, cleaned, lifted, hauled, dragged, hauled, muscled, sweat, and stank.

Phil more than the rest of us. He was in a hurry to get this stuff loaded so we'd get to the dinner stop as early as possible and he might put in a little extra time with this newly blossomed love of his life. We all laughed about that too, but we also worked harder to get this rendezvous accomplished for our friend.

In good time we were loaded and headed down the highway with only one more chore before supper—gassing the truck. Well, this truck was a monster; we were hauling a mountain of gear, six passengers, maybe 20 canoes on a huge trailer, also full of gear, and the tanks must have held nearly 100 gallons of fuel. Phil counted on that as his one chance.

He figured it would take at least six minutes for that gas to run into the truck.

The truck stop where we always fueled for the long, provisionless trek across Nebraska's Sandhills was a fairly complete facility, with a coin-operated shower for truckers. Phil planned to get a shower in the minutes we were refueling. (The boss was a butt-head and would never have given him an extra two minutes for something as silly as romance.) Phil had the $1.50 in quarters in his hand so he wouldn't have to waste time getting change. Before the wheels of that truck came to a stop, Phil hit the pavement and was sprinting to the shower.

Only to find, we later learned from his lips, the crushing reality of a sign saying "OUT OF ORDER."

Phil's very life was in his own hands at this moment. It was that dire and he knew it. (Even more than the rest of us: He married Tami, they have three children, they own dogs.) His mind whirled. He knew, as a man, what Tami's reaction, as a woman, in the one hour he might have with her would be to his, uh, aura, which, I think is important to note, wouldn't have bothered any of the rest of us men, even in the confinement of a crowded truck for 10 hours. Something had to be done, and he did it.

To this day, what I saw this man do gives me goosebumps. I've seen my own dogs dig out a 20-foot trench 6 feet deep to get under a fence just to sniff a passing lady dog's faint trail in the air. I have seen cats fight their way through 15 other wild cats to get at one object of their affection. And I saw Phil Pfeiffer drop his quarters into the slot of a car wash and walk half naked through that hell of stinging sprays, flailing brushes, and automatic squeegees. All in the name of love. Forget Romeo and Othello and Don Juan. They were pikers. Phil Pfeiffer. Now, there is a hero of love.

At dinner that night he was clean and sparkling and sat in a booth with Fair Tami, off a ways from the rest of us. We respected his moment of privacy with her. Well, until I finally couldn't restrain myself and on my way to the cash register strolled past their booth saying only, to no one in particular, "Anyone else smell hot wax in here?"

THE FALSE GODS OF EQUALITY

The bottom line is, men and women should have equal opportunity. The notion that we are even remotely equal otherwise is downright goofy. Rampant egalitarianism is becoming the ruination of this country. And you're hearing that from a mad-dog civil libertarian, a card-carrying whoop-de-do member of the ACL&U. One of the reasons I left the teaching profession is that more and more students—kids 18 or 19 years old—got the goofy notion that what they think is as valid as what I think. It's not. I carried into that classroom 40 years more experience than they had, and 6 years more education, and probably even more brains than most. They have a perfect right to express their opinions, but that does not for a moment mean that their opinions have even a remote chance of being equal to mine.

Am I being arrogant here? I don't think so. Say you're sitting in the waiting room of your local hospital waiting for a little operation on a brain tumor that's been troubling you. Lucky you, you get to choose between two surgeons. One is 55 years old, has 20 years of education in the subject of brain surgery, and has performed this very operation 857 times before. The other guy has worked for two years at the local video store stocking shelves. He's 18 and is working on his high school equivalence but has had some trouble with the biology section.

Which one you gonna choose? They're both good Americans. Shouldn't their opinions be equal? Hell, no, they're not equal, and only a half-wit would think they are; but they are both free in this wonderful land to express their opinions about brain surgery.

This doesn't mean some of the kids who passed through my classrooms weren't smarter than me. Some were. Some were probably even quick enough that they picked up quite a bit of English lit or anthropology in the semester I had with them. But I don't think you could make a lot of money betting on the odds of a proposition like that.

I know this sounds a little like Mark Twain's wonderful narrative in his *Roughing It*, where he has one of his characters arguing that a buffalo can climb a tree because no one has ever seen one fall to the ground trying. I think this is described as an *ad ignorantium* argument—challenging an opponent to disprove an argument rather than proving his own. But I think I'm right in saying that, all things being equal, all things are not equal.

> *Woman's at best a contradiction still.*
> —ALEXANDER POPE

At least not everywhere. African tribal music incorporates multiple, complex rhythms, one on top of the other, with countless forms of musical instruments and harmonic techniques. Eskimo music has one instrument—the frame drum, and one rhythm (1/1!). There is even one song in the Eskimo repertoire asserting that it is the last song because all possible songs have been sung. Both musical systems are adequate to their cultures; to assert they are equal is absurd.

On the other hand, Aleuts almost certainly know a lot more about sleds, dogs, snow, seals, and fishing than Ibos.

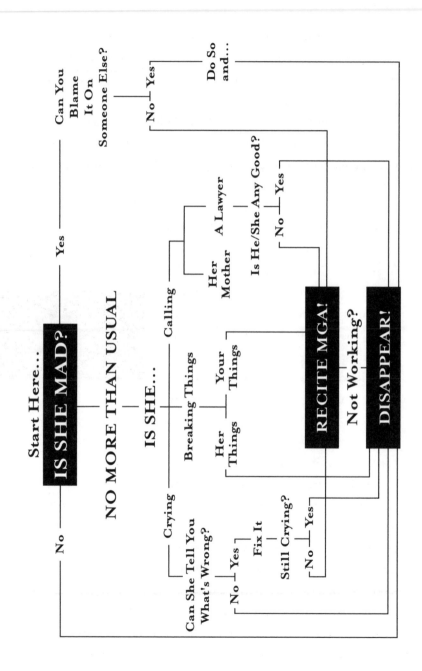

Start Here...

IS SHE MAD?

— Yes — Can You Blame It On Someone Else?

└ Yes — Do So and...

└ No

No

NO MORE THAN USUAL

IS SHE...

Crying

Calling — Her Mother   A Lawyer

Is He/She Any Good?

└ Yes

└ No

Breaking Things — Her Things   Your Things

Can She Tell You What's Wrong?

└ Yes — Fix It — Still Crying?

└ No

└ Yes

└ No

RECITE MGA!

Not Working?

DISAPPEAR!

An Allis-Chalmers HD-11 tractor could drag a Farmall Cub around the block sideways, no doubt about it, and when it comes to snaking cedar logs down a mountain road, the HD-11 would laugh the Cub into the ditch. On the other hand, that HD-11 sure would raise 69 kinds of hell pulling a basket cart through an apple orchard.

Of course women deserve exactly the same rights as men. Absolutely. They should get the same pay for the same work. Anything they can do, they should be able to do. Some women make better cops, firefighters, and muggers than some men, but not all women are exactly the same as men, just as not all men are exactly the same as women.

THE MALE GENERIC APOLOGY

If you know my name from anywhere, it's probably that Nobel Peace Prize nomination I got a couple of years back, in tandem with the Pulitzer Prize nomination, for my contribution to world peace, the Male Generic Apology. I attribute my own success in marriage, and with women in general, to a tattered copy of the Male Generic Apology (henceforth referred to in this study manual as "MGA"). I carry one with me in my pocket at all times. I've gone through several revisions over the years, but the copy I am looking at this particular moment reads:

> *Darling, I apologize from the bottom of my soul. I am sorry as I can be. I have no idea why I did something so stupid and insensitive. You know—I know, I was raised better than this. Tell me what I can do to make this up to you, as if anything could possibly make up for something this dumb. I swear I will do my best not to come even close to doing something this cruel again. You know I love you and only do*

*such things out of ignorance, never on purpose. Please
accept my apology. Let me take you out to supper tonight.*

[Note to craven apologizer: Hesitate at this point and
measure effect. If the object of the apology shows no sign of
relenting, say the following sentence, and only the following
sentence: "To some place other than Burger King." Pause.
Measure effect. In case of a continuing crisis, add, "and a
movie." In cases of clear and critical impending doom (say, she
is dialing her father), try, "you know, that great comedy about
the three women living in a city apartment who all get together
and spend the whole night having a fun pajama party talking
about their relationships." If it turns out she is dialing a lawyer,
play your trump card, as follows: "And then we'll go dancing."

If it gets any worse than this, to hell with it. There are
more fish in the sea.]

Laminate the MGA and carry it with you at all times. It
really doesn't matter what you have done wrong. Or that you
have done anything wrong at all. Although you can be pretty
sure that if you're a normal American male, you have almost
certainly done something wrong. The odds for this run very
high. Sort of like losing the lottery.

I have found it useful upon waking for the morning, right
after brushing my teeth and kissing the dogs, to stick my head
around the corner before venturing downstairs to the kitchen,
to shout the apology in the general direction of the women of
the house. That's why the address of the MGA is eminently
flexible: This same apology can be delivered to wife, girl-
friend, daughter, mother, house cat, or the witch behind the
counter where you pay your parking fines.

In fact, more and more I advise young men who come to
me for premarital counseling that they include the statement

in their wedding vows and thereby head off whatever problems are surely brewing. Like when she finds out exactly what went on at that bachelor party last night. The MGA is also now being included in a lot of premarital agreements. For example, in case of divorce, as determined by the laws of the state of [FILL IN THE BLANK] you get everything we own and most of what I hope to accumulate in the future, and Darling, I apologize from the bottom of my soul. I am sorry, blah blah blah.

One wrinkle I haven't ironed out of the MGA yet is that there are utterly unpredictable circumstances when it can bring a perfectly serene woman to fury. There is no explaining or predicting this. I am reminded of the time my first wife passed me by with a bowl of cauliflower explaining to the hostess at the dinner, "Roger doesn't like cauliflower."

"But," I sputtered in protest, "I've always loved cauliflower!"

"Well, I'm glad you changed your mind," she said without missing a beat, and still didn't pass me the cauliflower, by way of punishment, I rather imagine.

They learn this at Woman School, and they wouldn't want it any other way. Some brilliant anthropologist or another (I think it was George Carlin, but even if it wasn't, it should have been) said that a man gets married when he thinks this one is about as good as he's going to get; a woman gets married when she thinks she has something to work with. That's what they love, something to work with.

I think I first became aware of this during a field observation of the male/female relationship of primitive societies in a primitive corner of the world—our front room. It was early one Sunday morning and Woodrow dropped by as he often does to have a cup of coffee before setting out to secure meat for his family's table. Wearing the hunting outfit he'd had on since yesterday, and sporting the usual jaunty accessories of duck blood and feathers, hunting-dog spit, lake mud, plus a Cheez Whiz and braunschweiger sandwich, he sat down in Linda's favorite chair. I could tell from the look on his face something was troubling ol' Woodrow, so I diplomatically broached the subject: "You look like your best hunting dog just peed on your leg. What's going on?"

He then told me a story I've heard 18,563 times before, at least, in one permutation or another, the most basic exchange of the human male/female relationship. He said he got up that morning at the same time he gets up every Sunday and did all the same things he has done every Sunday morning for the 18 years they've been married. He put on his hunting (in other seasons, fishing) gear, made some coffee and sandwiches, and got ready to go out to face the world as it should be faced. Same old Woodrow, same old world.

Just as he was about to leave, he told me, his wife, Dottie, came into the kitchen, looked it over, looked him over, and then in a voice dripping with disgust said, and I quote women from over the millenia, "YOU'RE NEVER GOING TO CHANGE, ARE YOU?"

I could see it coming. Woodrow's question was Everyman's question since the dawn of time: "Change? Why would I want to change?"

See, he thought she had married him because she liked what he was, which is essentially what he still is. No. She married him because she saw something she could work with. Woodrow, like every other living man in all of recorded and unrecorded history, couldn't even grasp the nature of changing, let alone what things should be changed or what things he would want to change into. A black Lab doesn't wonder when he's lying out there in the grass on a nice Sunday morning, "You know, I could really improve myself by spending the day learning how to be a beagle." No, a black Lab is perfectly content to be a black Lab. Not because he thinks a black Lab is somehow superior to a beagle. Hell, his best buddy may very well be a beagle. No, he just can't imagine being anything other than what he is, or why he'd want to be anything other than what he is.

Woodrow loves Dottie, and he really does want her to be happy. He'd probably even change if he could figure out how. Or if he had any idea what changing is. I comforted him with a jigger of Southern Comfort and gave him a laminated copy of the MGA. Last I saw of him, he was headed out the door, driving his battered old Scout down the gravel road toward his duck blind, his dogs clustered all around him, muttering to himself, "Darling, I apologize from the bottom of my soul. I am sorry as I can be. I have no idea why I did something so stupid and insensitive. . . ." It was the best thing I could do for him. Really, the only thing I could do for him.

> *Of all the wild beasts of land or sea, the wildest is woman.*
> —MENANGER

Woodrow has since taken up the Roger Welsch School of Thought for Successful Relationships with Women. Even when he cleans up Dottie's kitchen to immaculate perfection after he and his buddies make venison jerky and drink three cases of Old Mil Lite in the process, he has learned to leave one cupboard door open and one dirty spoon in the sink. That way when Dottie re-enters her kitchen she can say disapprovingly, "Can't you ever leave the cupboard doors closed the way you find them? And look at the dishes! Whatever happened to cleaning up after yourself? Woodrow, you're never going to change, are you?"

And Woodrow just pulls the little card out of his back pocket and says, "Darling, I apologize from the bottom of my soul. I am sorry as I can be. I have no idea . . ." Works every time. Woodrow hasn't even had to go to the part about a movie, forget the dancing.

For all their protestations, women wouldn't want us to be any other way either. Worse than having something you can't work with is having nothing to work with, but don't try to use that as an excuse or apology. It won't work. Stick with the carefully worked out formula I have offered here, believe me. They aren't all that convinced that having nothing to work with is all that bad. I once came home from the tavern where a bunch of us had been discussing homosexuality.

I was pleasantly surprised to find that, here in the heartland of insensitivity, most of the guys in my circle of distinctly masculine friends demonstrated little or no hostility toward gay society. The prevailing attitude was mystification. Probably the most commonly expressed philosophical stance was "I just don't get it." Mick the Brick summed it up best: "I don't care what they do. That sort of thing is none of anyone else's business. But I, uuuuuh, well, er—I just don't want to know specifically what it is they do for fun."

I came home and reported the conversation to Linda, mostly because I was impressed by how thoughtful and tolerant everyone in this middle American, rural community seemed to be. I had to admit to Linda, in fact, that I, an educated liberal, found myself sharing their mystification. "You know," I told her, "I really don't get it either, not even lesbians, which usually strike males as less offensive than the male versions. I just can't see two women, you know, uh, being like, er, mates."

"Yes," she said after a moment's thought. "It really is hard to imagine. Coming home to someone who smells good, and doesn't need a shave, and whose clothes you can wear. Someone who knows how to sort laundry and can cook, and who likes line dancing and movies about relationships, you know, without explosions and car crashes, and who leaves the toilet seat down, and . . ." Well, she went on like that for about 15 minutes before I lost interest and drifted on out to the shop. You just can't talk philosophy with a woman, it turns out.

ALL MEN ARE PIGS

For those of us men who have daughters, the problem about male/female conflicts gets pretty sticky. Thing is, we know what men are like, and we know what women are like. And we want to protect our women children from other men's men children. And those of us who have men children want them to know about the ways of women. But there is no Man School, at least up until the publication of this book.

I turn to a handful of men I consider particularly accomplished raisers of children, Jack Davis, Woodrow, and Dan Gianneschi, who has a houseful of daughters much as I do, along with all the misery and confusion that condition implies. It was Dan's example I have followed in teaching Antonia, at the cue "All men are . . .," to spit out without hesitation, ". . . PIGS! ALL MEN ARE PIGS!"

Now, there is inevitably the problem and temptation when she eventually asks (and they all do), "Even you, Dad?" to say something stupid like, "Well, not your daddy, Sweetheart." That loophole is enough to screw up the whole exercise. No, admit what will eventually be evident to her: "Yes, Darling, even your daddy."

It's true, you know. How much better, more honest and wise it is, to simply admit it: All men are pigs. Do you know that pigs are very intelligent and actually fundamentally clean? They are. Did you know that pigs get bored quickly and easily? They do. Hog farms throw old bowling balls into hog lots, no kidding, to give the hogs something to play with, something to push around, something to think about. Sort of like me and, well, uh, old tractors and new tools.

The main difference between pigs and men is that hogs aren't very good predators. They just don't have to use a lot of strategy when it comes down to dealing with lady hogs because, well, they're both pigs, after all. In the case of human beings, only men are pigs. So, we have to have some other strategies in courtship and wooing.

I quote my tractor buddy Verne Holoubek's response to my query about the Easter dances on his home ground, in the Czech area of our state. I wrote to him, finding it curious that one would have a dance in celebration of an otherwise fairly gruesome church holiday.

He answered: "About those Catholic girls and Easter dances . . . big time in a small town. We were taught to fast and suffer during the Lenten season. Kids gave up chocolate or other favorites. By Easter, the girls hadn't danced or eaten chocolate for 40 days, and it was spring."

Draw your own conclusions from what Verne shared with me. As I said, hogs just aren't the predators that men are. That men *have* to be. If you were a woman, would you have anything to do with you?

A BETTER WAY

Some cultures have been more successful than others in working such things out. I spoke before about the terror-inspiring systems of polygamy in both native and immigrant cultures. Not even all Indians made that particular mistake. Take the Pawnee, the people who occupied the very ground on which I sit at this moment. Now, those guys had things worked out. Old men married the young women of the village, the theory being that old guys weren't going to waste a lot of the young ladies' time. They had some patience about certain things and had a special appreciation for the finer things. Conversely, older ladies got the young men because young guys really didn't care all that much just as long as the job got done, and the old ladies had also had the time and experience to develop an appreciation for the finer things under a buffalo robe.

That was a culture the much, much, much smarter white guys wiped out. The next time you visit your great-grandfather's grave, spit on it for me, okay? Ah, what might have been.

THE HIGHEST COMPLIMENT

A young lady who was about to marry a man (these days you have to include that kind of detail) came to me about a problem she was having with her fiancé. At least, she thought it was a problem. I think it was just a misunderstanding. It seemed that some things her future husband thought of as normal human physiological events struck her as rude enough that they threatened their future as man and wife.

I think you will agree with me that once again I approached the issue with moderation and the rare good sense you have come over the years to expect from me:

Actually, my dear, a fart is something of a compliment, a profound expression of trust. Think of it this way: Archie [an assumed name, but you could reasonably substitute the name of any male you know or are] is saying, "You've seen my best, and that's fine, but I think I can trust you to love me even at my worst, and here it is."

It's like a puppy rolling over and showing you his naked, pink, soft little belly, meanwhile peeing all over himself. He's saying, "I trust you not to hurt me even though I am utterly defenseless, because I think you are a good person. See how much I trust you?" A fart does that. It says, "We're in this together, Babe, you and me. No one else loves me enough to put up with something this disgusting, but I know you do."

Now that I think about it, when it comes right down to it, as it were, a fart is more romantic than roses and chocolates. Maybe that's the arcane meaning of the phrase "getting to third base." I have pretty much always known what getting to "first base" is, and "second," and, God knows, to "score," but I've always wondered about getting "to third base." This may be it. In fact, these days maybe third base is what a homer used to be and the ultimate achievement and commitment therefore is a four-bagger fart. No man farts in the company of someone he doesn't know, love, and trust. If women farted, they'd know that.

Earlier on, I spoke of the inherent and blessed differences between man and woman. It was no fool, although a Frenchman, who said, "Viva la difference." Any physical anthropologist can tell you a set of bones, even a small selection of bones, can usually be identified as male or female because we're different. It's not just a matter of slight variations in soft parts draped over identical frames any more than a John Deere B (an engine and transmission on a frame with wheels, sheet metal, and cooling, electrical, and lubrication systems) is identical to an Allis-Chalmers B (an engine and transmission on a frame with wheels, sheet metal, and cooling, electrical, and lubrication systems). Our jaws are different, our pelvises, and, apparently, our methane elimination systems.

In fact, my general experience and understanding of women is that they don't do anything that smells. Not just bad, but anything that smells. I think that's really nice. I don't know that I've ever smelled a woman. Oh, there's been Evening in Paris, Cheval Bleu, and Cabela's Special Superior Buck Lure, but never insofar as I know just, well, woman. But then I'm only 63 years old.

CHAPTER 11

TRACTORS,
WOMEN,
AND THE WEB

I'm not young enough to know everything.
—OSCAR WILDE

The most remarkable new tool I've seen come along in the world of old tractor collecting, repairing, restoring, and loving for the few years I've been in it is, without any question at all, the same thing that is changing life in general around the world—the worldwide web.

The world of the web came onto me pretty much like the world of old tractors. With tractors, I had owned and adored my 1937 Allis-Chalmers WC Sweet Allis for 12 years before the golden moment when I suddenly saw her not as an old and reliable friend but a love of my life, not as cold, rusty iron but as a living, glowing soul with personality and charm. Suddenly my life was changed.

I've been writing for more than 40 years now. The first book I wrote, *Treasury of Nebraska Pioneer Folklore*, is still in print to this day. It was published in 1966; I wrote it in 1964. And 1965, and 1966. I typed those 400-plus pages first on a plain old mechanical typewriter like you see in museums today.

I used carbon paper between four sheets of paper (if you are under 50, ask someone older what carbon paper is). When I made a typo, which is to say, about once a line, I stopped, rolled the multiple forms up, erased first the top sheet, then the second, then the utility paper, then the onion-skin foolscap, and then the last copy. Then I rolled it back down, positioned it, and hit the right key. If I was lucky. If I hit the wrong key, I repeated the whole process.

Four hundred-plus pages like that, and I did that three times until I had the manuscript where I wanted it. Next I took it to the University of Nebraska Press and they accepted it for publication, but it needed some changes. I typed it again. They liked the new version much better, but it still needed some changes. I typed it again.

Eventually I moved on to a Sears electric portable type-writer, and someone developed White-Out liquid correction goo, and then that thin yellow paper with dry white stuff on the back for correcting errors. Life was getting good for Ol' Rog.

Then I made a major investment in an IBM Selectric typewriter with a little moveable ball that flicked around and impressed letters on the paper. That was an advance with unexpected potential. Since there was no moving carriage to worry about, I figured out that I could run paper from a roller over the platen. I suspended a huge, heavy roll of shelf paper under my desk, ran it up over the back edge and into the platen, and then back over the rear edge of the desk; actually, a sheet of 3/4-inch plywood on four grape boxes.

Thing is, now I could type an entire book (350 pages) on a single sheet of paper for the first draft. Then I'd roll it up and do my reading and revisions. If I found a section here that I wanted there, I'd just cut it out with a pair of scissors, cut across the sheet where I wanted to insert it, and tape it all together again with Scotch tape. Wow! Now I was moving! Typing a book now took only weeks and months instead of years.

Then on the eighth day, God created the word-processing computer, and it was good. Man, was it good! Now it was just a matter of highlight, cut, flick, punch another button, and blocks of type were moved around with no trouble. With spell check, macro-changes, and fast scrolling, I felt like an Oregon Trail pioneer moving from a Conestoga wagon to a NASA space shuttle.

I accepted all those changes with enthusiasm; their potential was generally fairly easy to figure out. But when my daughter-in-law Beth showed me how e-mail and the web worked on her laptop computer during a Christmas visit here, well, yeah. It was cute, but I didn't really see how this silliness might pertain to me and my work or interests.

In a way, it didn't. That was four or five years ago, and in the world of the web, that is another Conestoga wagon-to-spaceship leap in technology. There wasn't much on the web at the time, and not many people were using e-mail. Now, I cannot imagine getting through an hour of my working day without the incredible advantage of this tool. It would be like trying to repair an old tractor without a single wrench of any kind—just pliers. You could probably do it, but man!

Okay, that's my work. I could go into a lot more detail about e-mail, but I won't. I'll save that for my love-romance-sex-marriage-and-computers book. But listen to this: Just this morning I was reading a note from a friend on the Antique Tractor Internet Service (ATIS) site who was telling me about his favorite web site and a story about his romance over the web. (I'll get to that later.) I noticed that his return address is, hmmm, not Pennsylvania, or Missouri, or Iowa, but THULE! He's at a base in Greenland, a place I've wanted to visit all my life. I now have a friend and correspondent in Greenland! And I can get mail to him instantly, and he sent me photos already this morning of an old abandoned and rusty International TD-18 crawler near his barracks. The communications potential of e-mail is absolutely stupefying. At least for this old dog.

But that's only a part of what "being online" can do for a tractor nut. There are tractor auctions, and parts lists, and talk lines where you can consult with real experts about the most exotic of problems. Engineers, mechanics, veterans, experts are at your very fingertips, and curiously eager to help the novice/idiot like me. The cost? By and large, nothing. That's right, nothing.

Yeah, you buy the computer and pay a small subscription price to be online, but mostly, the resources are mysteriously free. I have no idea how people make money out of these web sites, but I'm not going to ask too many questions as long as it's all out there for the taking.

Now this book is not just about tractors but about women and relationships too. While you may not have heard about all the tractor resources available on the web, you may have caught wind somewhere along the line of the, uh, naughty girl sites. Well, yes, there are plenty of those. I've heard. An amazing amount of them are also free for the ogling. Friends tell me. Perverted friends tell me.

There are some good girl things out there too. My favorite story is one I heard (or rather, saw) while researching this chapter. I asked various friends and the guys over on the ATIS site about their favorite tractor resources on the web, and I got a note from the guy in Thule, a good guy and frequent visitor to the ATIS site.

He wrote the following note:

> Good morning, Roger. There are some terrific technical resources out there on the web, but the sites that keep me coming back are the ones that give you a taste of the simple joy of rural life. I like storytellers, and perhaps more important, given the nature of your new book, women often like storytellers. So here are a few votes:
> • Chuck Bealke's Life on the Farm: http://web2.airmail.net/bealke/
> • Karl Olmstead's Old Tractor Page: http://members.xoom.com/kolmstead/
> • Mike Sloane's Home page: http://home.att.net/~msloane/
> • George Willer's Page: http://www.toledolink.com/gwill/
> • and my own, Dean Vinson's Farm Life Page: http://www.geocities.com/Heartland/Acres/4901
>
> I have some vague thought that I shouldn't vote for my own site, but hey, I like it. Hope you do too. Have fun.
>
> Dean Vinson

Well, that was nice, but I'm used to nice people in the world of old tractors. So I wrote back a fairly standard thank you:

> Thank you VERY much, Dean! Next I'll be soliciting opinions on sex, love, marriage, and romance!

And Dean replied:

> *You're most welcome. I've enjoyed a couple of your other books and am looking forward to the next one, and am delighted to help even in this small way. Can't help you with the sex part, but within the past year I've found love and romance with a dear friend from my long-ago high school days. Know what she saw that told her I'd become the kind of man she was looking for? My "Farm Life" web site. I'll get back to you next year about the marriage!*
>
> *Dean*

Isn't that sweet? Romance not only over old tractors but over the web! I mean, it's great that we can now locate parts, books, even whole tractors right from our work desks, but man, now we can even go courting without all that flowers and candy nonsense. Dean gave me the go-ahead to use the name of his Lady Fair: Dee Ferrell. Well, actually, Dee gave him permission to give me permission, and if that's not the start of a good ol' American marriage, I don't know what is. He's in Greenland and still asking the Little-Lady-To-Be for permission.

Dean, make sure you get started up there sorting the laundry right and leaving the toilet seat down. While you're up there with the walruses and icebergs, she's attending Woman School on a steady basis and getting that pretty head of hers full of notions about how she's going to "improve" you once the bill of sale is signed and notarized. You can count on that.

I would love to provide you with a list of web sites pertaining to old tractors (or, for that matter, nice girls like Dee or naughty girls like Boom-Boom Goodbody; not that I've ever actually visited a site like that, of course—it's just a hypothetical site I invented to make a point about the web, Linda). Thing is, whatever I would write today would be outdated by the time I shut this machine down and went into the house for supper. The worldwide web changes that fast, and almost always for the better and bigger.

A week ago I punched the word *tractor* into the Yahoo search engine. Now this is going to seem idiotic to anyone who has had anything to do with the web, I know, but indulge me here for the beginners, okay? A search engine (there are dozens) is just a place where you type in whatever you are looking for (IN THE WORLD!!!) and it will find whatever it can for you, which will more than likely be more stuff than you can sort through in a week. It is absolutely astonishing.

Every site you visit where someone has posted information about the subject you want to know more about is likely to have links; these are little buttons you move your pointer to, click, and off you go to another part of the world. It's dazzling.

Anyway, last week I put the word *tractor* into Yahoo, and listed for me (all for FREE!) the 531 different places I could call up on my computer screen

> *She thinks my tractor's sexy. . . . .*
> *She says it turns her on.*
> —KENNY CHESNEY,
> COUNTRY AND WESTERN
> WHINER

that deal with tractors. But get this: I did it again today just to check, and there are now 534 sites. By the time this book sees print, I wouldn't be surprised to find there are 1,000 sites for tractors.

I found only 4 sites listed for Allis-Chalmers, something of a surprise and disappointment, but there are 107 John Deere citations and, curiously, 513 for Minneapolis-Moline. None of that will be the same by the time you read this. But the bottom line is, with this easy, inexpensive device I am staring at, I have almost limitless access to more information, photos, facts, and opportunities than I can possibly describe to you. Or imagine for myself. I don't doubt for a moment that I will be surprised again the next time I take a flight on this thing called the web.

FRIENDS' AND FANS' FAVORITES

So you can see that any listing of sites for you to explore would be pretty silly. There's no way I can go look at all the sites; just not that much time in a lifetime. Not to mention that your interests are probably different from mine and in this biggest-in-the-world library, we need to go to the shelves that hold the books most interesting to each of our different curiosities.

I thought I would give you an idea of what your fellow tractor nuts are thinking. Here are some of the notes and letters I've received from friends and fans. Believe me, this is just a start, but it's a start that's been filtered through one layer of discerning web users. There is a place on a web page where you can save your "favorites," the pages you plan to return to again and again, so you don't have to retype the addresses for them again and again. (These things are sometimes hopelessly long and complicated, but if you have a site listed under your "favorites," you can move to it with just a flick of the button on your mouse.) Under my favorites there are the ATIS site (www.atis.net) and *Successful Farming* magazine's @g Online (www.agriculture.com). Going to these two sites is like walking into a gigantic supermarket full of goodies, but not for deodorant, disposable diapers, and school supplies. This store is full of your kind of stuff!

At the ATIS site you'll find discussion groups, bunches of men and women talking about exactly the kind of thing you want to talk about, and if they're not, well, you just jump in and pretty soon you're into the conversation and they are talking about the kind of thing you want to talk about. At the *Successful Farming* site, there is a trading post for machinery and parts, a section devoted specifically to old tractors (the sainted Dave Mowitz's Ageless Iron), and even an entire site devoted to your shop and tools—Top Shops. Just go to www.agriculture.com and start clicking on the buttons.

At the ATIS site, which is the work of Rust God Spencer Yost, there are auctions for parts, tractors, books and literature, collectibles, you name it. That site offers a list of other sites, and this is probably the best list I have seen in my experience. You just look at this list, click, and there you are—off on another adventure. Below is the ATIS site listing, but be sure to go there and check for yourself, because by the time this goes through the endlessly slow process of becoming a book, the web will have circled the world a billion times.

Appendices

Tractor Make and Model Links

AGCO's (Allis-Chalmers/Oliver/White) home page
Stratton Systems Unofficial Allis-Chalmers web site
Case IH's home page
Caterpillar's home page
John Deere's home page
Henk Hubers' Lanz Bulldog web page
New Holland/Ford home page
Gary Treible's David Bradley web page
The Unofficial Ferguson web page
The Unofficial Harry Ferguson web page
Drew MacPherson's Massey Harris web site
Tony Turner's Minneapolis-Moline home page
Kevin Coers' Oliver web site
John Ford's Rumely home page

Links to Antique Engine—Related Sites

Kelly's Elderly Engines home page
Harry Matthews Old Engine web site

Clubs and Resource Information Pages

Antique Gas and Steam Engine Museum web page, Vista, California
Buffalo Ridge Two-Cylinder Club's home page
EDGE TA's (Early Days Gas Engine and Tractor Association) web site
Farmers Hot Line web site (They specialize in maintaining information on agricultural equipment.)
FasTrac Antique Tractor home page
Historical Construction Equipment Association's web site
Larry Sikes' Florida Tractor Connection home page
Kate Smalley's Antique Tractor Resource web page

Norman O'Neal's Auction Ads web page
North Texas Antique Tractor and Engine Club web page
Old Engine.Org web page
Texas Agricultural Extension Service Clipart collection
Alan Moore's Serial Number web page

MANUALS, PARTS, EQUIPMENT, TOYS, AND COLLECTIBLES SUPPLIERS

Binder Books' web site (They specialize in providing manuals for IH equipment. They also carry manuals for AC, Oliver, and stationary engines.)
Classic Tractor Collectibles home page
Dennis Polk web site (auctions, parts, classifieds)
Fireball Heat Treating Company's web page
General Gear's Home page (has parts and services for only antique crawlers and the industrial variants of antique tractors)
JenSales (specializes in antique farm equipment manuals, sales literature, and toy replicas)
Heritage Equipment web page (John Deere toys, clothing, and collectibles)
Krem Enterprises web page
M&C Fayter's Steel Wheels
Ram ReManufacturing's home page (Ram specializes in the rebuilding and remanufacturing of engines from 1900 to the present and performs services such as babbitting, piston remanufacturing, and cylinder head welding.)
Tractor Buddies, Inc. web site (authorized dealer of WOODS brand mowers, rotary cutters, blades, and rakes for all makes of vintage tractors)
Yesterday's Tractors web page (Y. T. is a company specializing in new and used parts for pre-1975 tractors.)

PUBLICATIONS SITES

Antique Power's home page
Gas Engine magazine's home page
Green magazine's web site (a monthly publication for all John Deere enthusiasts)
Implement and Tractor Online web page
Successful Farming magazine's @g Online web site
Successful Farming magazine's Ageless Iron web page
Two-Cylinder Club web page
Tractor Tips web site (a web site dedicated to providing tractor tips to its visitors)
Western Producer's web page (*Western Producer* is published by Saskatchewan Wheat Pool)

My general request is posted at the ATIS chat page:

> *I am working on my next book for MBI Publishing Company, my long-prom-ised revelation of all my secrets about love, sex, romance, marriage, and uh, oh yeah, tractors. I can't believe no one's thought of that combination before. In previous books I told everything I knew about tractors. This time I'm spilling everything I know about women. (Whoops. There goes Linda with another of those terrible laughing spells of hers.) Anyway, I'm on the chapter about tractors and the Web. I need the advice of experts about tractors and the Web, not women. I'm doing a survey of the savvy guy's choices for the best, most interesting, most useful tractor web sites. What are yours?*

It brought forth these responses:

> *Date: Mon., 15 Nov. 1999 10:18:26 EST*
> *Subject: Re: Favorite tractor web sites*
>
> *Capt. Nebraska:*
> *Good to hear from you again! My first choice for tractor web sites is, of course, ATIS. My second choice would be Yesterday's Tractors. Another site I've found useful is Bigtoys.com, which is a heavy equipment web site. Looking forward to the new book!*
>
> *Regards,*
> *Karl Zinnack*

Karl was later corrected with a note that the "big toys" web address is actually a porno site! Other posters commented that, well, considering the topic of the book, it would fit in, as it were, either way.

> *Date: Mon., 15 Nov. 1999 10:28:48 -0500*
> *From: "Bryan Hartle"*
> *Subject: Re: Favorite tractor web sites*
>
> *Of course ATIS is the best, but I like the Unofficial Allis-Chalmers site as well.*
>
> *****
>
> *Date: Mon., 15 Nov. 1999 17:26:33 -0600*
> *From: Troy Burns Subject: Re: [Favorite tractor web sites]*
>
> *Roger,*
> *Write back when you get to the part about love, sex, romance, etc., etc., and I'll help you all I can.*
>
> *Troy*

Got several offers like that!

> *****

Date: Mon., 15 Nov. 1999 18:21:08 –0600
From: Jason
Subject: Re: Favorite tractor web sites

Here's one I stumbled upon: http://www.telusplanet.net/public/aharrold/
    A good start page, but if you click on Finding Old Iron: Harrolds' Antique Tractors and Engines you will find one of the best antique tractor links pages ever created. Or the direct link:
http://www.oldengine.org/members/harrold.

Jason DeJoode
Burnsville, Minnesota

Boy, this is a great one. I had it on my favorite places but lost it in the crash of 1998.

    ***

Skip and Betty
Palm Bay, FL
Date: Mon., 15 Nov. 1999 21:17:24 –0600
From: "goodwrench"
Subject: Re: [Favorite tractor web sites . . .]

    We obviously have a lot of agreement about the top commercial sites. As I mentioned when I first heard you were considering this project, I've put together a list of many folks' personal tractor-related home pages. I still have to add George Willer's and this would be a great time for other folks to let me know if I don't have your site. I'll be happy to get this all updated with as many as we can collect to give you a good complete resource.
    The current version may be found from a link at the bottom of my main tractor page, or it may be reached directly by going to:
http://www2.hot1.net/~goodwrench/lnktrthp.html.
    If anyone has a site they'd like to see added, send me a message and we can get Roger a great list.

Goodwrench

    ***

    Cook: Captain, I know you've gotten a lot of mail re tractor web sites, so I'll skip the common stuff and give you some more obscure things that I've found useful or interesting. Surely there is at least one thing in here you haven't found yet. Enjoy.

    Diamond Farm Tractors and Machinery book and video order—fairly complete and includes stuff not easy to find elsewhere: http://www.diamond-farm.com/diamondfarm/cgi-bin/diamondbooks.pl?1.

Binder Books—specializing in IH-related manuals and reprints but with some material for other makes as well, http://www.binderbooks.com.

Firestone Farm Tire Data Book—information on things such as hydroinflation for fluid ballast (putting water in your tires for weight): http://www.firestoneag.com/tiredata/index.html.

Pictures by Manufacturer—this is actually the ad page for calendars and videos, but if you quickly need to figure out what the heck a 1938 Avery Ro-Trak looked like, you might find it here: http://www.1webplaza.com/tractors/tracindx.html.

Texas Tractors—a web site/mailing list for talking about Texas and nearby tractor shows, auctions, etc.: http://www.egroups.com/list/texas-tractors/.

Tips for Buying a Used Tractor—a University of California Extension leaflet:
http://www.inform.umd.edu/EdRes/Topic/AgrEnv/ndd/faciliti/TIPS_FOR_BUYING_A_USED_TRACTOR.html

Viewit archive of photos and stuff—sometimes slow and hard to find stuff in, but also a good source for what various old tractors look like: http://acrux.astro.indiana.edu/pub/images/tractors/by-make. (It's particularly useful as a source of information for accurate restorations, such as this fine example: http://acrux.astro.indiana.edu/pub/images/tractors/by-make/farmall/luvchild.jpg).

Rust removal FAQ (mostly about electrolysis)—http://www.intricatearticles.com/personal/rustfaq.html.

Abrasive blasters and bead blasters—http://oldengine.com/abrasives.html.

Metalworking FAQ/Compendium—http://w3.uwyo.edu/~metal/.

I'll also include my own work-in-progress, http://www.farmall-h.com. focusing mainly on Farmall H stuff but the parts sources and other things are relevant to any IH tractor.

***

Greg Easely is an old friend and a good ol' tractor guy:

Besides YTMag and ATIS, I like mine,
http://www.geocities.com/Heartland/Woods/1416/
and a few of my other favorites are on my links page,
http://www.geocities.com/Heartland/Woods/1416/links.html.

Greg

***

My favorites are Darrin Stratton's www.allischalmers.com;
Yesterday's Tractors, www.ytmag.com;
and last, www.geocities.com/grandadsac/.
The last one may not be the quality you are looking for but I like it.
Thanks, Don

***

A fairly modest note from Phil Auten required a closer look:

Date: 15 Nov. 99, 16:44:16 CST
From: Phil Auten
Subject: Re: [Favorite tractor web sites]

Mornin' Cap'n!
Here's mine in order: ATIS, YT, Unofficial Allis, Brice Adams' image depot,
then a bunch of personal pages from mostly ATIS regulars, then a lot of pages for
parts dealers. Please feel free to e-mail me if you need something more specific on
the last two.
Phil

Okay, I bit and asked Phil for some details on his list.
Lots of guys have nice little lists; pretty much the usual
stuff, but sometimes there's a new piece of information in
there somewhere. Then I got Phil's list. Holy moley!!
Here it is:

ACMOC: http://www.acmoc.org/show/show.htm
Ag Equipment Salvage Yards: http://www.adeptr.com/agyards.htm
Agri Supply ® home page: http://www.Agri-Supply.com/
Alan Moore's S/N Reference: http://www.sckans.edu/~alan/tractor.html
American Small Farm: http://www.smallfarm.com/html/source_book.html
Antique Gas and Steam Museum: http://www.ziggyworks.com/~museum/
Antique Power, Inc.: http://www.antiquepower.com/
Antique Tractor Pulling: http://AntiqueTractorPulling.com/
Antique Tractor Resource Page: http://www.antiquetractors.com/
Antique Tractor S/N Reference: http://www.sckans.edu/~alan/tractsn.html
ASAE—Tractor Books: http://asae.org/pubs/history/index.html
ATIS Home page: http://www.atis.net/
ATIS Auction Site: http://www.atis.net/cgi-bin/auction.cgi
ATIS Chat: http://www.atis.net/Chat/ATISChat.html

Pretty impressive, no? Now, take another look at Phil's list.
That's not Phil's entire list; that's only the As from Phil's list! I
don't want to spoil the dramatic and heartwarming climax of

this book with Phil's whole list, but I want you to see it any-way, so I am going to put it in the appendix with Dave Mowitz's tractor list. When you finish this book, wipe the tears from your grateful eyes, and take a look at what these guys are sharing with us.

I know this is more than you wanted to know about the web, but I include all this stuff not so much for the incredible information source it is, but to give you an idea of what is happening on the web. This is precisely how it goes: You find a good source, and then it explodes like a puffball on a wet spring morning. Now you have hundreds of good sources.

The flat-out winner in my survey is the Yesterday's Tractors sites, variously listed as www.ytmag.com, www.yesterdaystrac-tors.com, and whatever this means, www.207.159.53.230/café.htm. This was even the favorite site of one of Tractordom's giants, Dave "Slo-Mo" Mowitz, who gets to the site using the address: www.ytmag.com.

No, actually, the flat-out winners are us folks who love old tractors. The days of sitting and staring at a busted or unidentified part and wondering what the heck we're going to do to figure it out are over. And isn't it one of those grand mysteries of the world that those of us who love old iron machinery are so totally involved in the cyberworld of silicone chips and electrons? (Speaking of good ol' Dave "Muddy Mo" Mowitz, I have added in the appendix Dave Mowitz's complete directory of international tractor organizations. It is an incredible resource, and I am very grateful to Big Dave for sharing this with us.)

I went to Lincoln not long ago to visit my parents. They're well up in their 80s, still trying to get used to the notion of airplanes and televisions, yet computers and the web. I told Mom I'd hook up my laptop and show her some of my favorite sites; a high-altitude view of our farm, a constant weather survey site, my son's articles in the Minneapolis *Star Tribune*, e-mail from my daughter in Seattle, our own home page.

"I just don't know, Roger," she sighed. "I really don't understand that computer and web and cyber stuff."

"Of course not, Mom," I reassured her. "I don't understand it either. In fact, no one understands it. It's just there, and it seems to work and anymore it's not even a matter of a luxury. It's something I can't live without. It's like magnetos and carburetors on a tractor, Mom."

I didn't say it out loud, probably didn't need to, but I was thinking, "Sort of like women, Mom. Sort of like women."

PHIL'S WORLD TRACTOR WEB SITES AND DAVE'S LISTING OF WORLD TRACTOR ORGANIZATIONS (MADE PUBLIC FOR THE FIRST TIME, RIGHT HERE, ON THESE PAGES)

The following is Phil's incredible compilation of worldwide web sites dealing with tractors. At least as it stood in December 1999. By the time this book winds up in your hands and you read all the way to this part, the list has probably exploded geometrically. Or disappeared. It's hard to tell about the web.

ACMOC: http://www.acmoc.org/show/show.htm
Ag Equipment Salvage Yards: http://www.adeptr.com/agyards.htm
Agri Supply ® home page: http://www.Agri-Supply.com/
Alan Moore's S/N Reference: http://www.sckans.edu/~alan/tractor.html
American Small Farm: http://www.smallfarm.com/html/source_book.html
Antique Gas and Steam Museum: http://www.ziggyworks.com/~museum/
Antique Power, Inc.: http://www.antiquepower.com/
Antique Tractor Pulling: http://AntiqueTractorPulling.com/
Antique Tractor Resource Page: http://www.antiquetractors.com/
Antique Tractor S/N Reference: http://www.sckans.edu/~alan/tractsn.html

ASAE—Tractor Books: http://asae.org/pubs/history/index.html
ATIS home page: http://www.atis.net/
ATIS Auction Site: http://www.atis.net/cgi-bin/auction.cgi
ATIS Chat: http://www.atis.net/Chat/ATISChat.html

Baileynet.com: Hyd. Cylinders http://www.cylinderquote.com/
Balcom Auction Calendar: http://www.citywideguide.com/balcom/baccalen-
    dar.html
Baldwin Filters: http://www.baldwinfilter.com/
Barnes and Noble: http://www.barnesandnoble.com/
Barnhill Bolt Company: http://www.BarnhillBolt.com/index.htm
Bates Corporation home page: http://www.batescorp.com/
Billy Joe Jim Bob's Truck and Tractor Links Page:
http://www.gunslinger.com/truck.html
Binder Books: http://www.binderbooks.com/
BLACKSMITH: http://www.loganact.com/mwn/bs.html
Books on Tractors and Farm Machinery:
http://www.countrylane.com/books/book50.htm
Brake Supply Company home page: http://www.brake.com/
Brillman—Old Ignition Parts: http://www.brillman.com/
Bulb Direct Catalog: http://www.bulbdirect.com/

Carter and Gruenewald: http://www.cngco.com/
Chain Quest/Tire chains: http://www.chainquest.com/
Chains—Tirechain.com: http://www.tirechain.com/
Chuck's TractorStuf: http://web2.airmail.net/bealke/tractors.htm
Classic Tractor Collectibles: http://www.1webplaza.com/tractors/tractors.html
Cockshutt tractors and Hercules:
    http://members.aol.com/Hobsickle/index.html
Cool Sites link: http://eagles.usit.net/tractor/Cool/Cool.html
Crossroads of Dixie: http://eagles.usit.net/tractor/tractor.html

David Bradley home page: http://www.cyberia.com/pages/gtreible/
ddc's Ferguson WWWebsite: http://home.rica.net/ddc3/
Dean Vinson's Farm Life page: http://www.geocities.com/Heartland/Acres
Des Moines Bolt: http://www.dmbolt.com/
Development of Stability Index for Tractors and Its Implication in Protective
    Structure Deployment :
http://lamar.colostate.edu/~jhliu/present_dis/index.htm
Diamond Farm Book Publishers: http://www.diamondfarm.com/
Directory of public images/tractors:
    ftp://acrux.astro.indiana.edu/pub/images/tractors/by-make/
Discount Tractor Parts and Manuals for Older and Antique Tractors:
    http://www.yesterdaystractors.com/store/index.htm
Dixie Sales—Lawn/Garden Equipment Parts: http://www.dixiesales.com/prod-
    ucts.html

Engine Oil Filter Study: http://minimopar.simplenet.com/oilfilterstudy.html

Farm Equipment Auction Farm Machinery Auctions: http://www.farmequip-
    mentauctions.com/

Farm Power and Machinery, Nebraska Extension Publications:
http://www.ianr.unl.edu/pubs/Farmpower/
Farmer's Webpage (Frobl): http://www.maxpages.com/robinsonco/
Farmweek: http://www.farmwk.com/
FasTrac—tractor resources: http://www.adeptr.simplenet.com/
Finding Old Iron: http://www.oldengine.org/members/harrold/

Genesee Products—Electronic Ignition for Agricultural and Industrial
Equipment:
http://www.ytmag.com/genesee/index.htm
Goodwrench's CyberRanch: http://www.CyberRanch.org/

Hall Farm: http://www.dialpoint.net/users/jeffhall/
Harrolds' Antique Tractors and Engines: related sites:
http://www.telusplanet.net/public/aharrold/eventrs.htm
H & H Trailer Company: http://www.hhtrailer.com/
HPOCA home page: http://www.hpoca.org/

Index of tractors: http://www.1webplaza.com/tractors/
Ingemar's home page—David Brown: http://www.canit.se/~ingemar/index.htm

JENSALES Tractor Manuals and Toys: http://dm.deskmedia.com/jensales/
Jet-Hot Coatings: http://www.jet-hot.com/

Ken Hough's Steam Traction Engines: http://members.xoom.com/tractioneng/
K&K Antique Tractors—Vynil Die-Cut Decals:
http://www.kkantiquetractors.com/

Lancaster Farming: http://www.lancasterfarming.com/
LeadFoot's OldEngine.Org unFAQ Page:
http://www.oldengine.org/unfaq/index.htm
LUBRICATION . . . a short course:
http://www.yondar.com/yondar/course5.html

Maine Tractor Crossing: http://www.mainetractors.com/
McMaster-Carr Supply Company: http://www.mcmaster.com/
M. E. Miller Tire: http://www.millertire.com/
Mike's Tractors—Parts and Tractors: http://www.mikestractors.com/
Minneapolis-Moline Corresponder: http://www.netins.net/showcase/corre-
sponder/mohr.htm

NASD Database: Documents by Topic: Machinery Safety: Tractors:
http://www.cdc.gov/niosh/nasd/menus/toptrac.html
National Automotive Lines, Inc.: http://www.natauto.com/
North Texas Antique Tractor and Engines: http://www.cyberramp.net/~ntex-
trac/
N. Texas Local Antique Engine and Tractor Activities:
http://www.cyberramp.net/~ntextrac/activity.htm
Nseries.com: http://www.nseries.com/

Oil Faq: http://vger.rutgers.edu/~ravi/bike/pages/pages/docs/oil.html
Old Engine.org home page: http://www.oldengine.org/
Oliver-Kline's Antique Tractors:
    http://members.tripod.com/~KlineAntiqueTractors/

Paynesville Tractor Parts: http://www.lkdllink.net/~ptparts/ptparts.html

Rock Ridge Farm—Florida Tractor Connection: http://www.gate.net/~lsikes/
Roger Welsch Home page: http://www.agriculture.com/welsch/roger/
Rummy's John Deere Page: http://johnnypopper.com/
RUST PRIMER: http://www.loganact.com/mwn/howto/rust/rust.html
Rust removal FAQ page: http://www.foxberry.net/dondon/rustfaq.html

Saginaw Tractor—3 Pt. Conversions: http://www.saginawcountytractor.com/
Sailbad's Homeport—Home of Sailbad the Sinner:
    http://www.angelfire.com/tx/sailbad/
Shorty Dear's Used JD Tractors:
    http://www.tractorsonline.com/equipment/usedears.html
Small Parts Co.: http://www.smallparts.com/
SSB Tractor Parts: http://www.ssbtractor.com/
Steiner Tractor Parts: http://www.steinertractor.com/
Stemgas Publishing Company: http://stemgas.com/
Stephen Equipment Antique Farm Machinery and Tractor Page:
    http://users.aol.com/glaq/antique.htm
Surplus Tractor Parts Corporation: http://www.stpc.com./
Swap Meet Home page: http://www.cnweb.com/swapmeet/

Texas Tractor Shows, Antique Tractor Shows, Tractor Pulls, Tractor Swapmeet:
    http://www.freeyellow.com/members/George56/page2.html
The Mower Parts Site Index: http://www.mower-parts.com/index.htm
The Northern Great Plains: Implements Used on the Farm:
    http://lcweb2.loc.gov/ammem/award97/ndfahtml/ngp_farm.html
The Perry Company, Waco/Temple: http://cust.iamerica.net/perryco/index.htm
Thomas Register of American Manufacturers:
    http://www3.thomasregister.com/index.cgi?balancing
Top Shops from Successful Farming: http://www.agriculture.com/topshops/
Tractorama: http://www.mountvernon.net/tractor/
Tractorboy's Home page: http://www.geocities.com/SiliconValley/Vista/1214/
Tractor Classifieds—ADEPTR: http://www.adeptr.com/ads.htm
TractorLinks.com—Mega Site of Tractor Related Links: http://www.tractor-
    links.com/
Tractor Parts Direct: http://www.tractorpartsdirect.com/
Tractor Tips—Select a Tractor Make:
    http://www.tractortips.com/threads/index.html
Tractor Web: http://www.tractorweb.com/
TRACTORWORKS Antique and Classic Tractors and SPEEDEX Equipment Sales:
    http://www.ns.net/users/gene/
Trader Online—classified ads: http://www.traderonline.com/
Tucker's Tire Company: http://www.tuckertire.com/
T. W. Cook: http://xtdl.com/~tw/

Vevay, Indiana Antique Tractor Parts:
http://www.venus.net/~rmartin/index.html
Voyles Brother Equipment—Salvage Tractors and Combines:
http://www.ytmag.com/voyles/index.htm

Walt's Tractor Parts, LLC: http://www.waltstractors.com/
Weber's Tractor Works (NOS IH PARTS): http://www.weberstractorworks.com/
Welcome to MTD: http://www.mtdproducts.com/
Western Minnesota Steam Threshers Reunion: http://www.rollag.com/
Western Montana Antique Power Association: http://www.cybernet1.com/old-iron/links.htm
Wiring the GM 10SI Alternator: http://www.oldengine.org/unfaq/10si.htm
Worthington Ag Parts: http://www.worthingtonagparts.com/

Yesterday's Tractors—farm and tractor books: http://www.olympus.net/tractors/bookcat.htm
Yesterday's Tractors—parts query form:
http://www.olympus.net/tractors/query.htm
Yesterday's Tractors—Pre-1975 new and used tractor parts: http://www.olympus.net/tractors/

ALLIS-CHALMERS LINKS

Allis-Chalmers All Crop Harvester page:
http://www.apocalypse.org/~jbvb/faf/ac_66.html
Allis-Chalmers Manual for Model WC:
http://www.iupui.edu/~harrold/ac/wc.html
Allis-Chalmers—Unofficial Home page: http://www.allischalmers.com/
Dick Harrold's AC Page: http://www.iupui.edu/~harrold/ac/
Fred Wilke's Tractor Lane: http://www.netrax.net/~wilke/
Grandads Old Allis-Chalmers Rest Home:
http://www.geocities.com/Heartland/Shores/2378/
Grove Equipment (AGCO Parts): http://www.groveequipment.com/
Yesterday's Tractors—The Little A-Cs: http://www.ytmag.com/articles/acbook/
Yesterday's Tractors—A-C Discussion Group: http://www.ytmag.com/ac/www-board1.html

I-H FARMALL LINKS

General Notes on the Farmall M:
http://www.geocities.com/Heartland/Acres/4901/about_m.html
IH Farmall Tractors by Jeff Grodey: http://members.iquest.net/~jgrodey/tractor.htm
IH Tractors: http://falcon.fsc.edu/~craymond/
Farmall H Information: http://www.farmall-h.com/
Farmall H Specifications: http://xtdl.com/~tw/tractor/Farmall-H.htm
Yesterday's Tractors—Farmall Discussion Group: http://www.ytmag.com/farmall/wwwboard.html

I can't imagine trying to assemble Dave's list of international tractor organizations, and I am not aware that it has appeared anywhere else. Dave Mowitz, machinery editor at *Successful Farming*, is a nice guy and a patron saint of us old rustbusters. He is really generous in sharing this list. This sort of data-rich text is outdated the moment it is printed, of course, but this is as close as we can get, and I am grateful to Dave for his generosity. And he is such a cute little rascal.

ADVANCE RUMELY
Rumely Collectors News
Scott Thompson
12109 Mennonite Church Road
Tremont, IL 61568
309/925-3925

Rumely Product Collectors
Ron and Lora Lea Miller
15525 Lake Road
White Pigeon, MI 49099
616/483-9282

ALLIS-CHALMERS
Old Allis News magazine
Nan Jones
10925 Love Road
Bellevue, MI 49021-9250
616/763-9770
Fax: same

The Allis Connection magazine
Cheryl Deppe
8480 225th Ave.
Maquoketa, IA 52060

Upper Midwest A-C Club and newsletter
22241 200th St.
Hutchinson, MN 55350
fax: 320/587-6923
e-mail: accLub@hutchtel.net

B. F. AVERY
B. F. Avery Collectors and Associates
Avery–Wards–General–M-M Avery
R.R. 1, Box 68
1373 E./100 N.
Paxton, IL 60957

J. I. CASE
J. I. Case Collectors Association
Old Abe's News magazine
Dave Erb
400 Carriage Drive
Plain City, OH 43064
614/873-3896
e-mail: oldabe@usa.net

Case Heritage Foundation
Heritage Eagle magazine
P.O. Box 081156
Racine, WI 53408-1156
414/554-5205

CATERPILLAR
Antique Caterpillar Machinery
Owners Club
10816 Monitor-McKee Road N.E.
Woodburn, OR 97071
503/634-2474 (M-F, 8-5 PST)
fax: 503/634-2454

COCKSHUTT
International Cockshutt Club
Cockshutt Quarterly magazine
Nick Jonknan
Route 2
Wyoming, Ontario N0N 1T0
519/899-2566

CUSTOM
Custom Club International News
Chris Proeschel
3516 Hamburg Road
Eldorado, OH 45321
937/273-5692

DAVID BRADLEY

David Bradley Newsletter
Terry E. Strasser
Route 1, Box 280
Hedgesville, WV 25427
304/274-1725

DAVID BROWN

David Brown Tractor Club
Champany Hill Farm
Silkstone Common
Barnsley, South Yorkshire S75 4PW
United Kingdom

EMPIRE

Empire Tractor Owners Newsletter
Carl Hering
5862 State Route 90 N.
Cayuga, NY 13034
phone: 315/253-8151
fax: 315/252-2108
e-mail: www.hering@dreamscape.com
www.sound.net-~dchering

FERGUSON

The Ferguson Club and Journal
Sutton House, Sutton
Tenbury Wells
Worcestershire WR15 8RJ
United Kingdom
(0584) 810424

FORD

Ford/Fordson Collectors Association
645 Loveland-Miamiville Road
Loveland, OH 45140
phone: 513/683-4935
fax: 513/683-1210
e-mail: www.ford-fordson.org

9N-2N-8N-NAA Newsletter
Gerard and Bob Rinaldi
P.O. Box 275
East Corinth, VT 05040-0275

GIBSON

Gibson Tractor Club and *ADEHI News*
Dave Baas
4200 Winwood Court
Floyds Knob, IN 47119-9225
812/923-5822

HART-PARR/OLIVER

The Hart-Parr Oliver Collector
Association
The Hart-Parr/Oliver Collector magazine
P.O. Box 685
Charles City, IA 50616
phone: 515/228-5406
fax: 515/228-5131
e-mail: hpocacc@fiai.net
web: www.hpoca.org;

INTERNATIONAL HARVESTER

IH Collectors Association
310 Busse Highway, Suite 250
Park Ridge, IL 60068-3251
phone: 847/823-3612
fax: 847/683-0207
e-mail: ihcclub@aol.com

Red Power Magazine
Daryl Miller
Box 277
Battle Creek, IA 51006
712/365-4873 (evenings)
712/365-4669 (days)

The Scout and International Motor
Truck Association
4683 W. 100 South
New Palestine, IN 46163
317/861-5364

Harvester Highlights
Darrell Darst
1857 W. Outer Highway 61
Moscow Mills, MO 63362
314/356-4764 (after 6:00 P.M.)
e-mail: buzzys@nothnbut.net

KECK-GONNERMAN

Keck-Gonnerman Antique
Machinery Association
Don Julian
5005 N. Ford Road
Mt. Vernon, IN 47620
812/985-7578
e-mail: jdjulian@evansville.net

John Deere
The Green Magazine and *The Swap Meet*
Richard and Carol Hain
2652 Davey Road
Bee, NE 68314
402/643-6269
e-mail: Grnswap@cnweb.com

Two-Cylinder Magazine
P.O. Box 10
Grundy Center, IA 50638-0010
web: www.two-cylinder.com

LANZ
Lanz Owners Registry
A. M. Watson
Willow Corner, Main Street
Marston Grantham
Lincolnshire NG32 2HH
United Kingdom
101540.1554@Compuserve.com

Der Pioneer
Lanz-Bulldog-Club-Holstein
Britta Jargstorff
An der Bundesstrasse 22
25358 Horst-Hahnenkamp
Germany

MASSEY-HARRIS-FERGUSON/WALLIS
Massey Collectors Association
Dale Lawrence
13607 Missouri Bottom Road
Bridgeton, MO 63044
314/291-7453
e-mail: dalemca@hotmail.com

Massey Collector's News and
Wild Harvest magazine
Box 529
Denver, IA 50622
phone: 319/352-5524 (evenings)
phone: 319/984-5292 (days)
fax: 319/984-6408
e-mail: Keitho@sbt.net

Twin Power Inc.
Box 429
Hagersville, Ontario N0A 1H0
905/768-1211

MINNEAPOLIS-MOLINE
The Minneapolis-Moline
Collectors Club
Dan Shima
409 Sheridan Drive
Eldridge, IA 52748
319/285-9407

M-M Corresponder magazine
3693 M Avenue
Vail, IA 51465
712/677-2433

The Prairie Gold Rush magazine
Ken Delap
17390 S. SR 58
Seymour, IN 47274
812/342-3608
web: kdelapmm@hsonline.net

RUSSELL
The National Russell Collectors
Association
561 29th St. N.W.
Massillon, OH 44647
330/833-6493
e-mail: steamgauge@aol.com
web: www.russellcollectors.com

SHEPPARD
Sheppard Club
Lynn Klingman
6775 N. Etna Road
Columbia, IN 46752

SILVER KING
Silver Kings of Yesteryear Tractor
Club
The Sky Writer newsletter
Leon Hord
4520 Bullhead Road
Willard, OH 44890
419/935-5482

ANTIQUE TRACTOR PULLING
National Antique Tractor Pullers
Association
Ed Epperson
5070 Weaver Road
Germantown, OH 45327
937/855-4326
www.natpa@eppersontire.com

The Hook magazine
Box 16
Marshfield, MO 65706
phone: 417/468-7000
fax: 417/859-6075
e-mail: thehook@pcis.net
web: www.pcis.net/thehook

STEAM TRACTION ENGINES
Iron Men Album
Linda Weidman
41 N. Charlotte St., P.O. Box 328
Lancaster, PA 17608
phone: 717/392-0733
fax: 717/392-1341
e-mail: stemgas@pptnet.com
web:www.stemgas.com

Live Steam magazine
2779 Aero Park Drive
Traverse City, MI 49686

Frick Engine Club
9161 NC Hwy #22
P.O. Box 220
Climax, NC 27233
336/685-4253

GARDEN TRACTORS
Vintage Garden Tractor Club of America
1804 Hall Street
Red Granite, WI 54970

Shaw Du-All Registry
22 Nesenkeag Drive
Litchfield, NH 03051

Gravelys Forever
7092 Hunters Ridge Drive
Plainfield, IN 46168
317/839-6869

Panzer Tractor Owners Club
Susan Heller
P.O. Box 2601
Manassas, VA 20108

Little G Lawn and Garden Tractor
Collector's Club
13306 Black Hills Road
Dyersville, IA 52040

GENERAL TRACTOR
MAGAZINES
Antique Power Magazine
Patrick Ertel
Box 500
Missouri City, TX 77459
800/310-7047
e-mail: antique@antiquepower.com
web: www.antiquepower.com

The Belt Pulley magazine
Kurt Aumann
20114 IL Route 16
Nokomis, IL 62075
phone: 217/563-2612
fax: 217/563-2111
e-mail: beltpulley@ccipost.net

Engineers and Engines magazine
Don Knowles
2240 Oak Leaf Street, P.O. Box
2757
Joliet, IL 60434-2757
815/741-2240

Gas Engine magazine
Linda Weidman
41 N. Charlotte St.
P.O. Box 328
Lancaster, PA 17608-0328
phone: 717/392-0733
fax: 717/392-1341
e-mail: stemgas@pptnet.com
web: www.stemgas.com

Polk's Magazine
Dennis Polk
72435 SR 15
New Paris, IN 46553
219/831-3555
e-mail: DPE@Skyenet.net

Rusty Iron Monthly
Box 342
Sandwich, IL 60548
phone: 815/496-9267 (evenings)
fax: 630/553-2154
e-mail: rusty@indianvalley.com

Tractor Classics CTM
Box 489
Rocanville, SK S0A 3L0
306/645-4566
fax: 306/645-4376

Steam and Gas Show Directory
Linda Weidman
41 N. Charlotte St.
P.O. Box 328
Lancaster, PA 17608-0328
phone: 717/392-0733
fax: 717/392-1341

Rusty Iron Monthly
Box 342
Sandwich, IL 60548
phone: 815/496-9267 (evenings)
fax: 630/553-2154
e-mail: rusty@indianvalley.com

OTHER AGRICULTURAL COLLECTIBLES

Cast Iron Seat Collectors Association
Charolette Traxler
Route 2, Box 38
Le Center, MN 56057-9610
phone: 507/357-6142
fax: 507/357-6378
Corn Item Collectors Association
The Band Board newsletter
E. Eloise Alton
613 North Long St.
Shelbyville, IL 62565
217/774-5002
Cream Separator and Dairy Newsletter
Dr. Paul Dettloff
W20772 State Road 95
Arcadia, WI 54612

The National Association of Milk
Bottle Collectors
The Milk Route newsletter
4 Ox Bow Road
Westport, CT 06880-2602
phone: 203/227-5244
fax: 203/227-2206

Rural Heritage Magazine
281 Dean Ridge Lane
Gainesboro, TN 38562-5039
phone: 931/268-0655
e-mail: editor@ruralheritage.com
web: www.ruralheritage.com

Farm Machinery Advertising
Collectors
FMAC Newsletter
David Schnakenberg
10108 Tamarack Drive
Vienna, VA 22182
703/938-8606
e-mail:
schnakenbergdd@erols.com

Missouri Valley Wrench Club and
Newslettter
Virgil Saak
403 Polk
Baxter, IA 50028-1019
515/227-3193

Spark Plug Collectors
The Ignitor magazine
Chad Windham
3401 N.E. Riverside
Pendleton, OR 97801-3431
phone: 541/276-4069
fax: 541/278-6169

Midwest Tool Collectors
Association
The Gristmill magazine
Wlliam Rigler
Route 2, Box 152
Wartrace, TN 37183
phone: 615/455-1935
fax: 615/455-0029
e-mail: billybob@edge.net
web: www.MWTCA.ORG
Windmillers Gazette

T. Lindsay Baker
P.O. Box 507
Rio Vista, TX 76093

The Happy Pig Collector Club
P.O. Box 17
Oneida, IL 61467

England Seat Collectors
David Cook
Harrowdene Paddok
Felmershan, Bedford MK43-7HL
England

CONSTRUCTION
Historic Construction Equipment
Association
Equipment Echos magazine
P.O. Box 328
Grand Rapids, OH 43522
phone: 419/832-4232
fax: 419/832-4034
web: www.bigtoy.com

TRUCKS
American Truck Historical Society
Wheels of Time magazine
Larry Scheef
P.O. Box 531168
Birmingham, AL 35253-1168
phone: 205/870-0566
fax: 205/8770-3069
e-mail: aths@mindspring.com
web: www.aths.org

This Old Truck
Patrick Ertel
Box 562
Yellow Springs, OH 45387
800/767-5828

The Scout and IH Truck Association
4683 W. 100 South
New Palestine, IN 46163
317/861-5364

The Antique Truck Club of America
Double Clutch magazine
Hope Emerich
P.O. Box 291
Hershey, PA 17033
717/533-9032

Power Wagon Advertiser
Dept SL 3090 Benton Iowa Road
Norway, IA 52318

Vintage Power Wagons
302 South 7th Street
Fairfield, IA 52556

The Willys Club
795 North Evans Street
Pottstown, PA 19464

ENGINES
Briggs-Straton Club
Jim Miller
Box 465
Conover, OH 45317

Maytag Collectors Club
Nate Stoller
960 Reynolds Ave.
Ripon, CA 95366
209/599-5933

ENGLAND
Tractor and Machinery magazine
Farm and Horticultural Equipment
Collector
Peter Love
Kelsey Publishing Ltd.
Kelsey House
77 High Street
Beckenham, Kent BR3 1AN
United Kingdom

The Ferguson Club and Journal
Sutton House, Sutton
Tenbury Wells
Worcestershire WR15 8RJ
United Kingdom
(0584) 810424

Vintage Tractor magazine
Allan Condie Publication
Merrivale
Main Street
Carlton, Nuneaton
CV13 OBZ
United Kingdom

David Brown Tractor Club
Champany Hill Farm
Silkstone Common
Barnsley, South Yorkshire S75 4PW
United Kingdom

Lanz Owners Registry
A. M. Watson
Willow Corner, Main Street
Marston Grantham
Lincolnshire NG32 2HH
United Kingdom
101540.1554@Compuserve.com

GERMANY
Der Schlepper im Ruckblick
Kurt Hafner
Kaiserbacher StraBe 34
71540 Murrhardt
Germany

Der Pioneer
Lanz-Bulldog-Club-Holstein
Britta Jargstorff
An der Bundesstrasse 22
25358 Horst-Hahnenkamp
Germany

SWITZERLAND
D'Fettpress
Freunde alter Landmaschinen Der
Schweiz-Fals
Paul Muri
Blumenweg
CH-5722 Granischen
Switzerland
0041-62-8421064

AUSTRALIA/NEW ZEALAND
Vintage Farming magazine
Alan T. Lewis
Racine
61 Boston Avenue
Christchurch, 8004
New Zealand
phone: 064-03-349-8073

Vintage Tractor and Machinery
Association of Western Australia
Lesley Smith
Box 43
Mukinbudin 6479
West Australia
phone: 0896851261
fax: 0896851359

Tracmach Newsletter
P. and V. Wifney
Box 32
Wyalkatchem
West Australia 6485
phone or fax: 0896811251

The Olde Machinery Mart
TOMM Magazine
P.O. Box 1200
Port Macquarie, NSW 2444
Australia
02 65850055
tomm_magazine@hotmail.com

SOUTH AFRICA
Vintage Tractor and Engine Club of
South Africa
The Veteran Farmer Magazine
The Editor
P.O. Box 8667
Centurion
Pretoria 0046
Republic of South Africa
0334-71405

INDEX